SMASH

YOUR ALARM CLOCK

LIVING THE DREAM THROUGH
REAL ESTATE INVESTING

JASON BUZI

Co-Founder of *Hidden Cash*

A POST HILL PRESS BOOK
ISBN: 978-1-68261-049-7
ISBN (eBook): 978-1-68261-050-3

Smash Your Alarm Clock!:
Living the Dream Through Real Estate Investing
© 2017 by Jason Buzi
All Rights Reserved

Cover Design by Quincy Avilio

Post Hill
PRESS

Post Hill Press
posthillpress.com

Published in the United States of America

TABLE OF CONTENTS

INTRODUCTION:
WHAT THIS BOOK IS ABOUT

In 2005, I was sitting in a tiny apartment, unemployed, broke, and in debt. I wasn't sure what I should or could do next. A mortgage business I'd been working so hard to build had been very good to me during its normal boom cycle, but was quickly going bust.

My income—once up to $20,000 in a month—had evaporated to zero, along with my savings. My credit wasn't great and I owed thousands of dollars to a friend.

Having a master's degree in economics might have helped me find a corporate job, but I'm a born entrepreneur who couldn't hold a traditional job for more than a few weeks.

In 2001, I'd gone to Taiwan to teach English for a year and a half—a great experience, and the only stable "job" I've ever had—but it wasn't what I wanted to spend my life doing.

Having a decent place to live in, a dependable paycheck, and a very stable job were appealing; every time things had gotten bad, my mind tended to wander toward the possibility of going that route again.

Asian countries—Taiwan, China, Japan, South Korea, and others—have a huge demand for native English speakers to teach English to their kids, teenagers, and businesspeople.

But somehow I'd turned 34 without losing my love of ideas and creative solutions. I had bought and sold cars and diamonds, operated a 1-900 (pay-per-call) dating service, and even tried my hand at professional sports betting. Sooner or later they'd all flopped, so I'd been reduced to temp jobs such as bookkeeping (glorified data entry).

At that point, my greatest successes had been as a mortgage loan officer and teaching English in Taiwan. I was forced to admit to myself that both were essentially dead-end careers without long-term benefits for a guy like me.

Foreign travel was appealing, but ESL teachers as a group weren't happy about living in a small room in a faraway country while old friends had acquired families, careers, and houses. Most felt unable to ever fit in back home or be fully accepted in an adopted country.

So what, exactly, were my options as my time and money steadily disappeared?

Just then, a friend of mine and newly minted real estate agent happened to buy a house to remodel and resell.

"I dont have money or great credit, can't fix or build anything, but want to get involved. What can I do?" I asked him persuasively.

"Find a house that's not on the market," he suggested.

Where should I look? I asked, and he suggested a couple of areas without explaining *how* to do it.

Before you finish reading this book, you'll know 100 times more than I did after that first conversation.

Remember that I hadn't taken any course, attended a seminar, or even read a single book on real estate investing—all of which I strongly encourage you to do, by the way.

Yet, within a few months of that conversation, I'd somehow managed to earn about $100,000 in real estate!

How? By starting to ask real estate agents if they knew of any off-market deals (which you'll soon be able to do too). Within weeks, I had my first deal.

Once I'd found a house, all I needed was a buyer—I lacked the money to close on the $975,000 San Francisco Bay-area house myself. Soon I was able to find a buyer, assign them the contract by "wholesaling," and walk away with a check for $25,000.

Having never even seen a check that big before, I was on cloud nine. So of course I kept doing it until I was earning around $250,000 to $300,000 a year wholesaling houses.

I wish that was my happy ending. Unfortunately, that party ended in 2008. The market changed and a worldwide recession started. But that's no excuse for failure.

Many people did even better in real estate during the recession. However, by not having built my business properly, I wasn't one of them.

I had limited myself in terms of areas, types of properties, the people I was selling to, and how I was investing in real estate. This made my business model very precarious.

By 2010, I was broke again. With no income coming in, and having just gotten out of a long-term relationship, I escaped for months in Asia on borrowed money and without even a tiny apartment to call my own. I was renting a motel room by the week and owed about $100,000. I didn't know what to do. Real estate seemed to be another dead end.

I didn't realize that "warehousing" was such a limited type of real estate in terms of area, types of properties, clientele, and how I was investing in real estate. My business model was unsustainable.

Some of my eye-opening experiences from 2010 will be discussed later. But as I sat in a motel room, I only knew that I was broke, in debt, and had no money coming in. So I told my parents about my struggles, and asked for money. My hardworking, middle-class parents had always been conservative and frugal financially, but I hadn't followed that example.

Being broke in your 20s is pretty much the norm. It is expected. Being broke in your 30s isn't great, but you're still young. After 40, it's just depressing.

When we reach rock bottom in an area of life, we have two choices: Stay there or use it as a motivator and a springboard to bigger and better things.

I try to do the latter in life, and suggest you do the same.

Now nearly 40, I had to beg my parents for money to survive. I vowed I'd never put myself in this position again.

I learned from real estate agents that there were still tremendous opportunities in real estate—there always have been, and always will be.

But I had gotten lazy. I stopped the marketing and networking I should have been doing. I never went beyond "wholesaling" and never owned or closed on a single property in my own name.

On top of these big mistakes, I hadn't been very smart with my money, and simply lost focus.

Who could have imagined, in 2010, when I was at such a low point financially and emotionally, that within a few years I'd be earning more than $1 million a year, buying a million-dollar house in cash, meeting the love of my life, and having a lifestyle most people only dream of? I did it all through real estate, and I have only barely scratched the surface of what's possible.

But don't confuse this with another book on real estate investing or house flipping. This is a book about lifestyle, about making money, but also having the freedom to live a more fulfilled and meaningful life. It's a book about having freedom to pursue your passions and interests, whether that's playing golf, spending all day at the movies, volunteering at an animal shelter, spending more time with your family, or traveling the world.

Studies show that having more money actually *does* make people happier, but mainly when we use it for experiences and to help others. It makes us less happy when we use it to buy things. Maybe that's why, although I love to travel and give back, I don't drive a Lamborghini.

I owe a debt of gratitude to all those who taught and encouraged me along the way. To real estate, and to the United States of America, which is still the land of opportunity.

Last but not least, to human resilience. We each have within us the power to turn our lives around at any moment. So let's get started!

1
OPEN LETTER TO A YOUNG PERSON

Note: Although this is intended primarily to be read by someone aged 15-30, it can benefit anyone. Having reached the ripe old age of 43, I was reflecting on all the mistakes I made in my youth, and what I would tell myself, or someone in that same age group, if I could travel back in time. Here it is:

First of all: Congratulations! On what, you may ask? On possessing something that all the money in the world can't buy, and that millionaires and billionaires would envy you for and would probably be glad to trade places with you for: youth, and, presumably, health.

You are truly in the prime of your life. These are the best years. Decades from now, you'll look back longingly, as you'll miss this time and the youth which can never be regained. We all become nostalgic as we get older—some more than others. My hope for you is that you will not look back with regret. That's why I'm sharing this advice.

The good news is, these are the best years of your life. The bad news is, you are a fool, and will probably squander them. Hold on! Don't be so easily offended! I only mean that you don't yet have the wisdom and judgment that comes from age and experience, which you'll gain over time. In fact, your naiveté and ignorance may even serve you well at times, as the old can be too cautious.

But this is a letter to a young person, so let's not waste any of that precious time.

Shakespeare was right when he wrote, "To thine own self be true." Make this your guiding principle in all that you do. What does it mean exactly? Be sure that all your actions, large or small, are consistent with the person you are and want to be. More misery comes from not following this than from anything else. If you are true to yourself, you'll discover an occupation that suits your personality, pick a partner who suits you, act in a way that's consistent with your morals or ethics, and so forth.

It may sound obvious, but believe me, so many people take actions that are not consistent with who they are at the core—they pick the wrong job or partner, and act in ways they'll later regret. We have all done this at times, and usually regretted the consequences. So let "to thine own self be true" be your guiding principle in all that you do.

I will break down my advice into three broad categories: career and money, relationships, and "other."

First, let's talk about . . .

CAREER AND MONEY

Before you choose a career, do some serious soul-searching. Many people change careers several times over the course of their lives, but it's not an easy thing to do.

Begin with this fundamental question: Do you want to work for yourself or for someone else? Make a decision based on your personality and preferences. Do you need lots of structure? How important is stability to you? Do you crave camaraderie? If you answered "yes," you should seek a job working for someone else.

Conversely, ask yourself: Can you handle income uncertainty? Is freedom very important to you? Are you self-motivated? Are you creative? If you answered "yes," you should work for yourself.

"But what should I do?" you ask.

Let's start with anyone who prefers to work for others. Realize that there are few positions in the job market with much job security. Even traditionally secure jobs like teachers, police officers, and government workers have experienced waves of layoffs. If you prefer to work for others (which is not my preference) for heaven's sake, at least make sure the job is secure.

As I mentioned, there are only a handful of secure jobs, with very low unemployment or attrition rate. Currently, these include: medical doctors, nurses, math and science teachers, government attorneys, software engineers, teaching English overseas (been there, done that), and a few others. As these change over time, be ready to do your own research and find a job that pays well *and* is secure.

Keep reading, though. I have some financial tips for you too.

For anybody who prefers to be self-employed, it's a wise choice that I can thoroughly relate to. But before you pat yourself on the back, prepare to face many years of struggle, sacrifice, and poverty before you finally "make it." That's because you are not as smart as you think you are.

Of course, *you* think you're smart. And maybe you are. But you still lack the judgment and experience needed to make the right decisions, and you'll still fail time and again until you get it right.

Let me make a two-word suggestion: real estate. I tried more businesses than I care to remember throughout my 20s and early 30s—Internet marketing and selling cars and selling diamonds among them—until I finally discovered real estate at age 34. I've made more money in a short time than with all those other businesses combined. There is nothing like it, unless you are exceptionally brilliant and lucky and have a knack for technology, and are the next Sergey Brin (Google) or Mark Zuckerberg (Facebook).

And, realistically, what are the chances of following in their footsteps? For every success story there are hundreds, if not thousands, or even hundreds of thousands, of failures. So many variables have to fall into place, and everything has to work perfectly, to make it happen. And technology, competition, or legal changes can wipe out any business in the wink of an eye.

Twenty years ago, travel agencies were a good business. Fifteen years ago, pay phones were a good business. And 10 years ago, bookstores were a good business. What will be the next to go?

Real estate has remained, and will always remain. The advantages of real estate are boundless. And no capital of one's own is needed to get started in real estate—something I wish I'd understood many years ago.

For those who want to work in a job or are interested in another business, I still recommend real estate as an investment, if not a full-time business. It has created more millionaires than any other activity when they bought properties as a side business, either flipping them, or holding them as long-term rentals. So at least start educating yourself on real estate by buying a few good books on investing. James Lumley's and Robert Shemin's books are excellent primers.

When it comes to money, always live at least a little below your means, and save! Following this advice would have spared me a lot of heartache and struggle during some tough times. And try to accumulate assets, not only cash, by creating multiple streams of income if possible. These could be interest from bonds, dividends on stocks, other business income, or rental income from real estate holdings.

Do your best to own your own home, without overleveraging yourself to do so. Make a large down payment or buy it with cash.

Finally, for the artists and the dreamers: You do not want a "job." Nor do you want to be an entrepreneur. Therefore, you deserve a category of your own. You are following your passion and your dreams of being a musician, writer, actor, stand-up comedian, or painter. Just be honest enough to admit that the odds against your success are probably 1,000 to 1, whatever your level of talent.

Too many talented people must work as waitresses and bartenders, dreaming of their big break. Visit L.A. sometime and talk to some of them as they refill your drink.

It is very important, as I've said, to live a life without regrets, so *do* pursue your dreams. But put an expiration date on them: three years, five years (probably ideal), or longer. And work it 110% for those years. Then, if you don't "make it" by then, be practical and pursue a more realistic occupation with which you can support yourself and have a solid future.

At least three of my close friends have all done this. They pursued creative careers and failed, and now have other jobs and are in their early 40s.

Whichever category you fall into, be true to yourself, and carefully consider something which utilizes your talents, interests, and skills, without neglecting practical considerations such as success and income potential and job stability. Weigh the emotional against practical considerations.

RELATIONSHIPS

In general, you should discover exactly what and who you want without getting married young. The longer you wait, the more likely you are to become a person who knows what you want from life—and from a partner specifically.

Why not spend your 20s and into your 30s dating different people? If you want children, though, don't wait too long! Mid- to late 30s would be the time to get married, in that case. Once past 40, your stamina and energy levels inevitably decline. Do you really want to be raising children into your 60s? Think about that.

If you're in a committed relationship, do your best to make it work. Treat him or her right. Talk nicely to them. Men, bring her flowers occasionally. Take her to a nice dinner or a play sometimes. Tell her you love her. Be kind to her. Compromise. The more love you give, the more love you'll get back. Love him or her with all your heart, and have a happy life. Don't jump ship at the first sign of trouble. Try to work things through. Apologize when you need to. A person who is shown love and appreciation and kindness on a regular basis is much less likely to stray or walk away.

LIFESTYLE CHOICES

Travel the world. Spend some time living and working in a foreign country. For Americans and other native English speakers, there are plenty of jobs abroad teaching English or doing various things. You'll experience many eye-opening adventures. You might spend a summer volunteering abroad through Volunteers For Peace (vfp.org) or a similar organization. Look into it.

Formal education, generally speaking, is somewhat overrated— unless you get the right degree from the right school. A Yale law degree, Stanford engineering degree, or Harvard business degree will open many doors. A bachelor's in psychology from Chico State? Not so much.

This book is also about making smart and practical choices, if you don't plan to be an entrepreneur. Be sure you go to the right schools and get the right degrees for the right professions.

College can be a great social experience, so I do encourage you to go and at least get a bachelor's, if you can afford it, even if you *do* plan to be an entrepreneur. It didn't benefit me in any direct way, but was a nice experience. I made some friends, and liked being "educated."

Try to do some volunteer work, and if you have a few extra bucks, donate to those less fortunate. Help out at a soup kitchen, or a nursing home or at a shelter for battered women, or a hospice for children with terminal illness. You will gain better perspective on life and realize how blessed you are.

Good friends are hard to find. The word "friends" is used very loosely. For example, I now have more than 700 Facebook friends, the majority of whom I have never met in person. Many others I haven't seen in years, although we live less than 50 miles apart. And yet, we call these people "friends."

Don't forget what *real* friendship is. Real friends will be there for you through thick and thin. They'll help you through hard times and celebrate your good times. They will visit you in the hospital and lend you money if you ever need it. They share in your sorrows and joys, and give you advice when you ask (if not always good advice, at least well-intentioned). Anyone with two or more friends like this is very lucky. If you have more than 10 such friends, we are not using the word "true friend" the same way.

And read! Always strive to learn something new. Read for pleasure, too—about the world, other ways of thinking, or anything of interest. Formal education may be overrated, but informal education is seriously *under*rated.

Think critically and independently. Even if you belong to a political or religious or social organization with strong principles, don't lose your sense of self. Remember that no one is *always* right. Think for yourself.

Have at least one hobby. Life is not all work. It's good to have a few outside interests, whether it's tennis, bowling, or knitting.

Appreciate your health! This is almost certainly the healthiest you will ever be. Don't take it for granted. Health problems will become bigger issues and concerns every year after about 40. Take care of yourself as much as possible. Without telling you to eat right and exercise when I am not always doing that myself, I hope you don't take good health for granted.

As for religion: No advice here, except it seems to be important to so many people, and surveys show that it usually makes people happier. Follow your heart, but don't forget your mind. Live a balanced life. If you need a spiritual component, discover what works for you. I personally don't believe everyone needs to be spiritual or religious to be balanced. Conversely, many religious or spiritual people are very unbalanced or immoral. As I said, find what fills your heart in this sphere.

Don't hold grudges and be judgmental. Think about reaching out to someone you haven't spoken to in years. Don't let anger weigh down your heart. Move on to a new chapter. It's never too late.

AND REMEMBER

Live without regrets! Always, "To thine own self be true."

Best wishes in creating the life of your dreams. Don't forget to enjoy the present moment. These will soon be the "good old days."

Be grateful for what you do have! Some of the happiest people I've met were among the world's poorest in Ghana, West Africa. Some of the most miserable were wealthy people I met in my business.

However old you are, if you are still breathing, remember—it's not too late to change your life, and start living the dream!

All the best to you!

2

REAL ESTATE

JASON BUZI'S 10 RULES FOR SUCCESS IN REAL ESTATE:

1. Positive attitude is a *must*. I could dwell on all the deals that didn't work out and all the challenges of being self-employed. But instead, I focus on opportunity and possibility. There has been a lot of doom and gloom recently. However, this is still the land of opportunity.

2. *Focus!* This is even more important than hard work. I'm lazy. I spend most days at the park, at cafes, at movies, and elsewhere. But I have put systems into place to generate potential deals on a regular basis. And when there's a deal, I'm like a shark, like a bulldog. I bite and don't let go without a fight. If there is a way to make it work, I make it work!

3. Don't deal with flakes. Associate (in business) only with people who are successful or have the right attitudes to become successful. (Also beware those who overpromise and under-deliver. But I guess that's about flakiness too).

4. Use multiple strategies for getting deals.

5. Use massive and consistent effort. Don't expect meek and weak efforts, or occasional efforts, to yield any impressive results on a regular basis.

6. Become an expert in your market, and learn to adapt to changing markets and different market and property types.

7. Be *smart greedy*, not dumb greedy. Smart greedy = trying to maximize your profit on each deal through negotiation (the most profitable activity known to mankind), deal structuring, cost controls, and so forth. Stupid greedy = taking foolish risks, cutting corners that shouldn't be cut, destroying relationships for short term gain, and so forth.

8. If any *one* deal, agent, client, investor, et cetera, can make you or break you, you've put yourself in an overly vulnerable position. Don't put all your eggs in one basket.

9. Business, like life, is filled with ups and downs. Try not to let either affect you too much. That said, do reevaluate and readjust as needed if you are not getting the results you desire. First review one through eight, and ask which you could be doing better.

10. Always aim higher! Demand and expect more from yourself than anyone else would.

Recently, I attended a real estate seminar in Las Vegas. The main topic of the real estate conference was cash flow. Cash flow investors are focused on generating as much money per month as possible for every dollar invested, and often try to use creative strategies to achieve it. They're not as interested in making a quick $100,000 (or $500,000) by flipping a house, as I am.

I also think cash flow is important. This is why I own rental properties, where the money comes in every month like clockwork. It's a beautiful thing. But I am not going to pass up quickly wholesaling, double closing, or rehabbing a property and earn from $50,000 to $500,000—usually in a month or less.

So, at this cash flow conference, I ended up meeting someone from the Bay Area. I noticed on his name badge, he's from an upscale small town adjacent to me. Since people at the conference were from all over the country, I felt it gave us some connection.

I introduced myself, and told him we were neighbors. He told me he lends money to a guy in Pennsylvania, and invests everywhere else because "there are no deals in the Bay Area."

Now, I agree that cash-flowing properties is much harder in the Bay Area, but I proceeded to tell him about a house I just sold a couple days earlier, one I rehabbed and made $120,000 on, less than five miles from where he lives.

By the way, I also competed against five other investors for that house, including a HomeVestors franchisee. It never went on MLS (multiple listing service), but they called the people who sent letters. I asked if the agent would represent me and she wouldn't, so I did the next best thing: I had her best friend represent me. I did a quick, 30-day, $55,000 rehab and walked away with $120,000 profit, more than many people earn in a year.

It always astounds me how otherwise intelligent people say "there are no deals" in a certain area. Really? My deal was in the next town over from him. This guy had just sold his house for $3 million, so he couldn't be that stupid. But he insisted: "There are no deals in the Bay Area."

When I gave him the full details of my deal, his only reply was, "Well, if the market had gone down, that house wouldn't cash flow." In other words: assuming one put 20% down, the rent would not cover the mortgage.

Maybe not, but it would probably be pretty close, and should I pass up $120,000 on the small chance that the market will crash during my 30-day holding period? It made no sense. But he was so fixated on "cash flow investing" that he claimed "there are no deals in the Bay Area,"

13

despite the fact that myself and many others made millions there. He was attending conferences in Las Vegas, and investing for peanuts in Pennsylvania, but had no interest in making six figures per deal in his own backyard. It's fine with me, one less competitor. But it really makes no sense.

Recently, I met some remarkable people who are doing real estate in a way that has led me to reevaluate how I run my business. One gentleman I befriended lives in San Francisco, because he thinks it's the greatest city in the world (he may be right), and wholesales houses in Memphis, TN—a market 2,000 miles away.

Every time I look at Facebook, he is traveling with his family in Croatia, Puerto Rico, Japan, etc. He recently quit his full-time job, and his wife is about to quit hers. He makes about $50,000 a month wholesaling, and the remarkable thing is that it is all virtual. He has two virtual assistants in the Philippines making offers for him, and he has a lady on the East Coast talking to sellers (he tried having someone in the Philippines do that too, but sellers responded better to a fellow American).

The only part of the business he handles is selling the property once it is under contract. The offers, conversations with agents and sellers, and visits to the property are all outsourced to other people. He could even outsource selling the property, but he has chosen to do this himself.

Last month, he assigned seven properties and made about $7,500 each, on average. He makes in a month what many people earn in a year, and doesn't risk any money, and has lots of free time.

In February 2016, I went to Arizona and sat in a mastermind group with some of the biggest coaches in wholesaling: Sean Terry, Justin Colby and Kent Clothier. They are some of the biggest names in their fields. They have written books and host seminars and popular podcasts. They have built seven-figure businesses wholesaling real estate "virtually," using acquisition specialists to negotiate with sellers (doing either outbound calls or inbound calls from their marketing pieces), disposition specialists to help sell the properties to investors, and so on.

I also went to Florida to meet with Mark Evans, DM ("The Deal Maker"), one of the most successful "turnkey" operators in the country. He works in multiple markets across the Midwest and South, buys cheap houses, fixes them up, puts a tenant in, and sells them to "cash flow" investors, looking for monthly income. He has people specializing in talking to sellers and negotiating to buy their homes, repair crews and property managers in each market, and people who specialize in selling the properties to investors. He runs everything from Florida, and is often yachting in the Caribbean or traveling the world while his business continues to bring in millions a year in profits.

What my new friends have shown me is something that sounds like a fantasy. You can make millions in real estate and have it be a totally virtual business. You do not have to be physically present to meet and negotiate with sellers, agents, or buyers, or view any properties yourself. This is not how I run my business now (I *do* meet with sellers, agents, buyers, and view every house before I make an offer), but it's definitely possible to do.

Real estate can get you anything you could ever want or need financially. Just be careful to choose the right property and process. Broadly speaking, there are three financial objectives that real estate can satisfy. These are the three financial needs of any person. Of course, there is plenty of potential for overlap, but there are three financial objectives:

1. Fast cash *now*.
2. Long-term asset accumulation.
3. Residual income.

If you think about it, that covers all financial needs, and all of these are possible with real estate.

1. **Fast cash *now*:** This is what wholesaling is all about. Make some fast money, get a four- or five-figure (usually) check today.

2. **Long-term asset accumulation:** This is when you buy property and either put enough down or have enough built-in equity—or both—so that you have an asset that is worth more than you paid for it. And, hopefully, it will continue to appreciate. It can also be achieved by taking profits from real estate and investing them elsewhere, including in having six or seven figures in cash equivalents (checking/savings accounts, CDs, money market, and so forth).

3. **Residual income:** This comes from owning rental property, being a private money lender, or holding a note. A real estate investment that pays you monthly (or quarterly or weekly or even daily) dividends. Most often this refers to owning rental properties.

Items **2** and **3** often go together. If there's a house or fourplex that's worth $500,000 and you got it for $300,000—and you plan to keep it long-term—you're probably not going to let it sit there vacant. You will probably rent it out. The question is: What is your key objective? And what should it be long-term?

Item **1** is a hallmark of an *immature* and unseasoned investor. Hold on! Don't be so sensitive. That was also me for the first half of my investing career. Circa 2005 to 2008, I was making good money, only wholesaling, getting a nice five-figure check every four to eight weeks. I was pulling down about $250,000 to $350,000 a year.

Then the crisis came. My savings were quickly depleted. I had no real assets. I had zero residual income. With my savings done, I went into debt.

Then I did what every mature, responsible person in my position would do: I fled the country. I spent nine months traveling the world. I had some great times, but I really didn't know what the future held for me. The financial news coming out of the United States in 2009 was not encouraging.

I came back home, and long story short, began my comeback in 2010. From 2010 to 2013, I was smarter, and although I needed fast cash *now*, I also started thinking more strategically about my long-term financial future.

As soon as I could, I started saving and buying property myself. I went from a real estate wholesaler to a real estate investor. Closed on properties in my own name. Partnered on others for equity stake. Started seeing six-figure, not only five-figure, paydays. And only in 2014 did I finally hit objective 3: Holding properties for long-term residual (rental) income.

That's been my progression from 1 to 2 to 3. And I'm still doing all three. I wholesale for fast cash. I invest long-term. I have residual income goals. All of these things. *But*—and this is important—my mind-set is dominated by 3, and to a lesser extent, 2. I have clear goals in terms of monthly residual income, and somewhat more vague goals on amount of assets.

Those monthly residuals will make me financially free. And that's the maturation process. If your mind-set is solely on 1, you need to look ahead. I was stuck there too long. And I'm kind of slow. The journey from wholesaler to investor to owning rental properties, which took me nine years, could and should have taken half or a third as long. But we all grow and learn at a different pace, and in different ways. Whatever you do, make sure your mind is looking five or 10 years down the road, not only at today and this month.

This section is dedicated to those kindred spirits who are dreamers, like myself, but also willing to take action to make their dreams come true. I hope that is you.

"The reason most people don't truly succeed in life is they major in minor things. They focus on what seems urgent rather than what is truly important."

–Tony Robbins

"Most people get too caught up in making a living to design a life."
–Tony Robbins

"Your life can change in an instant. The instant a decision is made."
–Tony Robbins (I like the guy!)

"Failing to plan is planning to fail."
–Alan Lakein

"There are always opportunities."

–My dad

"Anyone can become financially independent through real estate in five years, but it won't necessarily be their first five years."

–Mike Cantu

"I don't know where I would be without you, but I know it wouldn't be a good place. I really can't imagine my life without you. I have tried others. All have failed and disappointed me. Only you have been true. We had our moments of doubt and struggle, but our love is now truer and stronger than ever. You've allowed me to fulfill my potential and be the person I was meant to be. Everything I have is, literally, thanks to you. I love you, real estate!"

–Jason Buzi

3

HOW TO GET RICH

I assume you want to get rich. Almost everyone does. Who would prefer to rent a small apartment than to own a nice house of their own? Or to drive a crappy car instead of a nice one? Who wouldn't want to take vacations when and where they want? Who wants to worry about bills? Who wants to have to work for or with people they can't stand? Okay, we agree that almost everyone wants to be rich. Yet few make a real attempt at it.

Let's figure out how to get rich.

There are basically four ways (not counting inheritance, lottery, and the like, as those are just a matter of chance, not career or business plans):

1. You're extremely talented as an artist, a sculptor, painter, actor, writer, musician, comedian, and so on. Or athlete. Guess what? So are a million other people. With a lot of hard work, persistence, luck, and probably compromising your principles along the way, you might be that one in a million who makes it and beat out the 999,999 who think they're better than you. And a lot of them are probably right. Good luck.

2. Get a good job. Your best bet is to become a highly specialized physician, a profession I personally find distasteful (blood and guts? No, thanks). Like a heart or brain surgeon. After high school, you will need four years of college, followed by another four years of medical school, followed by about four to eight years of residency to specialize. You'll probably have a massive amount of debt. But you will make a mid-six-figure income. After 10, 15, or 20 years, you can retire relatively wealthy.

   You can also go to law school or get an MBA, although there are lots of unemployed attorneys and MBAs around. But if you go to a top school, and work at the right firm, you will make low six figures starting out, and then maybe become a partner or senior executive and make mid-six figures or more. Then again, by the time you reach your 50s, you should be wealthy.

3. Start a business. Invest a lot of time and money into it. Whatever business it is, the odds are against you. It's a well-known statistic that 80% to 90% of new businesses are shuttered within five years. A new technology or competitor or change in the economy could decimate your business overnight. You have to do almost everything right to succeed, and even then, there are countless factors outside your control. But maybe you will be one of the lucky ones, your business will thrive and make you rich, or you will get bought out. Again, good luck.

4. Get into real estate. You don't need any specialized skill, education, training, or degrees. There's a lot of free or very inexpensive information out there showing you everything you need to get started. You don't need any money or take any risks to start. You don't have to go into debt. People have made, and continue to make, money in real estate in all different markets and all over

the world. Your mistakes, which everyone makes along the way, can be corrected and you can strengthen your skills. Opportunity is everywhere and available to everyone. Since everyone wants to own one or more properties, and since every business needs real estate, there's always demand, and the possibilities are infinite. As a top investor put it: "Until shelter goes out of style, there will always be fortunes to be made in real estate."

So these are the four main ways you can get rich. I've made my choice, and it's working out pretty well (hint: it's not numbers 1, 2, or 3). I've tried 3 numerous times and never succeeded, by the way. Unless you consider success making a modest amount of money for less than a year.

I really believe that unless you're incredibly, extraordinarily talented in some field (be it basketball or biotechnology), real estate is the surest path to riches. Incidentally, even my brother, who *is* a doctor, has made far more from our real estate investments over the past five years than by practicing medicine, which he does full-time.

4

MY STORY AND THE NITTY-GRITTY DETAILS OF THE DEAL

(Or the most relevant parts at least, which may be illustrative and maybe even inspirational to a few of you. If I can get people to believe in themselves, even one person, I will have succeeded. The saddest thing to me are people who don't believe in themselves, and therefore do not even truly attempt to fulfill their potential.)

When I graduated from college with a master's degree in economics in my mid-20s, I had little direction, or even an exact idea, as far as what I wanted to do. Looking back now, I'm a born entrepreneur—selling cookies door to door at age 12, Cokes on the July 4th at 13, starting a telemarketing company at age 19, and so on. But, after college, I didn't know what I wanted to do, and real estate was the furthest thing from my mind.

I knew I needed a job (or thought I did—nobody actually needs a job. People need two things: purpose and money; most jobs provide both, but not very well), so I started sending out my résumé. I was disappointed at the lack of responses and it took me a few months to get a job.

When I couldn't find one right away, I did what I always do at a time of crisis: I left the country. Spent a summer in Eastern Europe, traveling and doing some volunteer work with a school in Poland. Came back and finally, got my first real "job" out of college. It was for a small credit bureau that provided merged credit reports. Their main clients were mortgage brokers. It was owned by a husband and wife. My job was supposed to be marketing/sales. The husband owner kept telling me how these mortgage brokers made loads of money. I started thinking "maybe I should look into that."

On the second day on the job, I was on the computer and supposed to be working, but I took a minute to check my personal e-mail. The wife happened to see me and flew into a rage. She started screaming at me that she was not paying me to check my personal e-mail. She was absolutely furious and yelling at the top of her lungs. It was crazy. This crazy, angry woman fired me on the spot.

I had a few experiences like that, but less dramatic. Shortly afterwards, inspired by my former boss, I entered the mortgage business, as a loan agent, and was very successful. For a while. Interest rates went up, and the calls stopped and I went from making $10,000 a month to zero literally overnight.

I wasn't very successful at it, and again, I did what I always do at a time of crisis: That's right, I left the country! This time I went to Asia and became an English teacher in Taiwan. I spent a year and a half there and came back home. Just in time to re-enter the mortgage business in my second refinance mania, when rates dropped and phones were ringing. This time, I was even more aggressive in marketing, and was making $20,000 a month. Good money back then, but it didn't last long. Rates went up, and business died in 2004. So what did I do? I left the country. This time, I went to Africa to volunteer at a library in Ghana.

As 2005 rolled around, I was sitting in my apartment, broke and in debt. The mortgage business was dead, and I didn't even know what it was like to have a real job. I still don't, and I doubt I ever will. Broke and not knowing what to do, I happened to have a friend who had recently become a real estate agent and was rehabbing his first house.

"How can I get involved?" I asked. "I don't have any money, my credit is iffy, I don't have any contractor skills, but . . . I am hungry and will use my pea-sized brain to try to make us money."

"Find a house off-market." He said. That was it.

"Where?"

He told me some areas he was interested in. He didn't tell me how to go about doing this.

I didn't read a book or attend a seminar. I put a system together that I still use. I found a deal, and three days later, walked away with a $25,000 finder's fee. This was the most money I'd ever seen. I had just wholesaled a house, though I didn't yet know that term.

I kept doing the same thing for the next few years, making a very healthy six-figure income. What you will know when you finish reading this section, and especially if you attend my class, will be far more than I knew when I started. I will also teach you things I only learned in the last two years, as I have taken my business from six to seven figures a year.

In 2008, the bottom fell out of the economy, and my business was one of its victims. First, the mortgage meltdown, followed shortly thereafter by the housing crash, and then the global recession. In hindsight, although I had been doing some things right, enabling me to earn about $300,000 a year for several years, I had made some critical mistakes, which I will be discussing.

One of the main ones (see my success principles in the next section) is I did not adapt and change with a changing market. My biggest mistake was I only being a wholesaler.

I wasn't a real estate investor until later. An investor, like I am today, will close on a deal when it makes sense to, will perhaps partner on some properties, can rehab if it makes sense, and may or may not wholesale. I still wholesale most of my deals, but I usually close on my best ones. Unless I can get a big enough fee to not bother with it, or I miscalculated (which happens and will be discussed).

Anyway, when it all went to hell in 2008, what do you think I did? Can you guess? That's right. This time, I took a six-month trip around the world, came back home for a bit, and then took a three-month trip to Southeast Asia from 2009 to 2010. Except for one deal in early 2008, I did no real estate deals at all in 2008 or 2009. I lived off my savings and then, I am sorry to say, got into debt.

In 2010, I made my comeback. I knew I had developed some skills, but also knew I would have to step up my game and do things differently—more seriously—and better, so that I would not make some money only to find myself broke a couple years later.

Upon reflection, I realized I'd done a few things very wrong:

1. I did nothing to adapt to a changing market. I could have gone after foreclosures, short sales, etc.
2. I was also way too limited in my area. I was only marketing to less than 5% of my potential market.
3. I had gotten comfortable and stopped networking. I was wholesaling most of my deals to two buyers. They were buying with stated income loans, meaning they didn't have to prove how much they made. In 2008, with the mortgage meltdown, those loans quickly went away, and so did my buyers.
4. I got overly generous by hiring friends in the business and overpaying them when someone could have done the same job

for half the price. I even made one a partner for a while. I'm not saying never partner with a friend, but this was not a reliable person. Big mistake. Fortunately, we are still friends.

5. I was frivolous with my money. I could and should have saved much more than I had. Enough to last me for at least five years. I distinctly remember having $100,000 in the bank at one point, and feeling like a rich man, and acting accordingly. Today, I don't even consider one million dollars in the bank to mean you're wealthy, even if it puts you in a better position than 95% of Americans. It depends where you live too. I live in the Bay Area, the most expensive real estate market in the country, and a place where you read about multi-millionaires and billionaires in their 20s and 30s all the time. If I lived in Ohio or Kansas, I might feel wealthier. Anyway, that $100,000 was gone within a year.

6. I lost focus. Just when business was slowing down, and I could least afford to, I lost focus. I brought a friend from overseas to help me, and we ended up spending more time hanging out than working. I started an unrelated Internet company, a field I knew nothing about. I lost tens of thousands on that experiment. I stopped marketing and networking as aggressively.

Then I hit rock bottom in 2010 and decided to make a comeback. I did a lot of soul-searching, realized my mistakes, and vowed not to repeat them. This is when I came up with my 10 success principles, which I regularly read to remind myself, and hope you will as well.

In 2010, I started looking for deals again by passing out flyers in a residential neighborhood in a nearby town that I'd never marketed to (another past mistake! too limited of an area). I got three deals there within months. I wholesaled the first one for $25,000. The size of that check was identical to my very first real estate check back in 2005. Like then, it was very emotional and could not have come at a better time, as I was completely broke. Like then, I hoped it was the beginning of something—in 2005 a new business, in 2010 my comeback!

And it was major, bigger, and stronger than ever. A few months later, I tied down another deal. I got it under contract for $875,000. I found an investor agent who agreed to buy it from me for $75,000 more. I was about to get a $75,000, badly needed, wholesale fee, when my brother heard about the deal and tried to persuade me we should do it as a family project.

After a lot of discussion, emotion, and argument, I finally agreed, and became a partner for the first time, not just a wholesaler. When we sold the house, two months later, we made a $400,000 profit, and my share was more than $100,000.

This got me out of debt and marked two firsts: The first time I had ever been a partner on a deal (I had only wholesaled up to that point), and, not coincidentally, my first six-figure profit on a single deal.

Many more such paydays followed and only one was from wholesaling. The others were from flips, rehabs, and partnering on new luxury construction projects. In a few years, I went from being broke to a real estate millionaire.

In addition to the home of my dreams, I now own multiple rental properties. Since I am conservative, I am not very leveraged. In other words, I like to own most properties either free and clear or with a lot of equity. I am sure I could have figured out some leveraged or creative way to control hundreds of apartment units or dozens of houses, but that's never been my goal.

This isn't bragging. I don't need to be the richest guy, stressed out and working 80-hour weeks, or the over-leveraged guy who risks losing it all with a 10% market correction but loves to talk about his huge portfolio.

To me, it's about financial freedom with minimum risk and maximum peace of mind. That means a few things, like making sure you'll make money on your deals before you buy, not buying and then hoping for the best. It means not buying with the assumption that the market will go up, but protecting your downside. I would personally rather own five houses with no mortgage than ten with a mortgage (assuming same equity position).

This is not to say that leverage or loans don't have their place, but I would advise you to be conservative. No one has ever gone broke by owning multiple properties in good areas free and clear. Many have gone broke overborrowing.

The market got tougher in 2012. Not crashing like in 2008—just the opposite. It got too hot. Newspapers were screaming headlines like "35 Offers On One House!" and "Bidding Wars Are Back!" and "Home Prices Breaking Records!" The number of short sales, which I had started doing just the year before, and had made a lot of money with, declined, as rising property values meant fewer sellers needed to do them.

Everyone knowing the market was hot meant that fewer owners wanted to sell off-market. Why should they when they could list their house and get multiple offers in one weekend and then sell way above asking price? They told me this and so did the agents. Response rates to my direct mail, already less than 1%, dropped even lower. A hot housing market tends to attract more agents and investors (including rookies), so I am sure competition was a factor as well.

Rookie investors tend to overpay, and rookie agents tend to overpromise.

Point is, it got harder to get deals. So what did I do? Did I quit? Did I leave the country? No, I decided to work harder and smarter, and to market more aggressively and better. The market did get tougher, but

I got better at what I do. Ever since my comeback, I knew there were too many deals I had wholesaled which I should have bought myself. I started doing that when an opportunity presented itself.

I bought a condo for $200,000 that needed no work. I resold it shortly thereafter for $320,000. I became majority buyer of a house for $975,000. Resold it a week later (no work) for $1.25 million. I rehabbed a house myself for the first time and made $140,000. I gained confidence and knowledge. I partnered on luxury home construction where the profits ranged from $1 million to $2 million (my take was a double-digit percentage of that).

Doing these things, and being better at how I do real estate, and improving in all three steps (which I will discuss soon) took me from broke to six figures a year to—for the first time in 2013, and every year since—seven figures a year. I've also been smarter about how I invest my money.

In 2014, I completed my biggest deal. I double-closed and made half a million dollars in profit on one deal. I got emotional about such a huge sum for me, and I daresay for most people. It marked another watershed moment. The timing was perfect. I was able to pay all cash for a duplex at $420,000, which is now rented for $4,000 a month, and worth at least $650,000 currently. I plan to keep it as a rental and a cash cow.

But I also wanted to give back to the community somehow. I felt it was time to do that. I gave some money to a few charities, but I wanted to organize something fun for people. I had an idea to recreate the TV show Survivor in San Francisco, having people do various challenges and the winner would get $5,000 or $10,000. I would advertise and finance it.

Why do it? The whole Hidden Cash story can be found later in this book

One of the best things about financial success is the ability to give back and do what I want, when I want. I truly wish the same for anyone reading this. And if you take action, and follow the steps and principles here, you can do it. Though, of course, everyone's path will vary.

I feel grateful for the opportunities I have had, and humbled and honored by the chance to share my story and lessons with you, and to call myself a teacher once again. Teaching is the only real "job" I ever had for any length of time, and I enjoyed it.

My success doesn't come from my intelligence or ability, but from the great opportunity that real estate affords to anyone without extraordinary skills or education. My success comes from the resilience of the human spirit.

And, last but not least, to this great country, where with determination and hard work, anything is possible. America is still the land of opportunity. People from all over the world come here for that reason. It's sad that so many Americans have lost sight of that.

In January 2013, I met with a very charming real estate agent who had a lovely British accent. We got together at a cafe and had such a good conversation that I decided to show her several homes I flipped, all of which I bought off-market at substantial discounts.

She seemed impressed. Then she dropped the bombshell: First, she said, I could have legal problems buying houses direct from sellers without an agent. I should use her to represent me, paying her commission for houses I find.

Then she said: "It's great what you've been able to do. But the market has changed. You won't be able to find off-market deals anymore."

And then she asked me if she could list the projects my partners were doing.

Haha, what?

No more off-market deals? I ended up doing 17 deals in 2013, all off-market, and for the first time, earned $1 million that year. I also bought my own house in 2013, with at least $300,000 in equity (none of my neighbors could believe the deal I got).

The agent was right that the market was becoming more competitive. But instead of quitting, I marketed more, networked more, and expanded my territory. I also tried to maximize my profit on every deal, not wholesale way-too-cheap as I had previously done.

The bottom line: Don't ever let anyone tell you that you can't do something. To hell with them. Prove them wrong! Success is the sweetest revenge.

THE THREE STEPS TO FLIPPING SUCCESS

There are *only three things* you need to get good at if you want to make a lot of money flipping houses. You do not need to know how to use a hammer, screwdriver, or paintbrush. You do not need a huge buyers list. You do not need a real estate license. You do not need a formal education or an above average IQ. Here are the three things you *do* need:

1. Learn how to generate leads on a consistent basis. Ideally, off-market properties that you can buy at a discount. Most of these leads will not make sense. Hence, you need to learn how to generate a lot of leads.

2. Learn how to quickly evaluate these leads. The good deals go fast, and you need to decide what's a good deal, what's garbage, and what goes in the "maybe" pile. I evaluate about 100 leads a month and end up moving forward on 1.5 of them, on average.

3. Learn how to structure the deal you move forward on for maximum profit. I was stupid, so I sometimes took $5,000 for a deal I could have made six figures on if I had structured it properly. I have also gotten $100,000 wholesale fees. I have double-closed and made six figures multiple times. Once you decide it's a deal, you need to use the strategy that will maximize your profit. I used to be just a wholesaler. Now, I am an investor. However, wholesaling is still a great strategy to use. However, make sure to measure the risk/reward of the various strategies, and not leave a bunch of money on the table.

Important: There are two other steps that aren't separate, but are prerequisites to this never-ending process of finding, evaluating, and structuring deals: market knowledge and networking with investors.

Obviously, you can't effectively evaluate leads if you don't understand your market. You can't do it by Zillow. Here are a few examples from my own experience, including two failures of my own:

KNOW YOUR LOCAL MARKET!

First example: In 2015, Zillow showed two properties as being worth about $1.2 million each. I got one under contract for $750,000. More than 35% below Zillow's estimate. Even the bottom-feeding lowballers would like those numbers, right? Well, I couldn't wholesale it to save my life, and ended up canceling the contract. Can you imagine if I had bought it with the hopes of reselling it for the Zillow number?

Around the same time, there was another property Zillow also showed as being worth $1.2 million. I tried to make an offer, but the owners didn't want to sell. I would have gladly paid $1.5 million for it. I'm sure I could have flipped it for an instant profit, and that its market value as is would be at least 50% above the Zillow estimate.

By the way, these houses were about 50 miles apart, but in different submarkets. And this is what made the difference. It had nothing to do with property condition.

Second example: I was driving through a suburb and saw two homes for sale. They were across the street from each other. I noticed that the bigger, nicer house, with a bigger lot, was selling for about $250,000 *less* than the smaller, less attractive house. I was dumbfounded until I learned that the nicer house went to a different and far inferior school district than its neighbor across the street.

Third example: In December, 2014, I canceled a contract because a property was facing a T-intersection. I learned it is bad "feng shui" and as the majority of buyers in this area are Chinese, no one wanted this development project. The Chinese thought it was bad luck, and the non-Chinese knew about it and worried about resale. Even with all my experience, doing hundreds of deals, and my closest partners being Chinese, I didn't sufficiently take this into account when I made my offer.

Fourth example: Consider two high-end markets, both in the Bay Area, about 30 miles apart. In one, lot size is everything and condition of the property doesn't matter much. In the other, condition is everything and lot size doesn't matter much.

No guru and no seminar and no book could teach you these local nuances. You have to study and learn your local market yourself. There is no substitute for that. And in every market you have submarkets and local nuances. Who are the typical sellers? Who are the typical buyers? What are the "hot" areas? What are the less booming ones? How much do schools matter, and which are the good ones? How much does lot size matter? How about house condition? What about cultural preferences like the one I just mentioned? What are some "deal killers?"

How do you learn about your market?

Talk to agents, and understand the paramount importance of DOM (average days on market).

I'm not the only investor who has a love/hate relationship with real estate agents. At times, we naturally find ourselves on opposite sides. It's their job to close as many deals as possible, whatever the outcome. It's my job to make sure the deal makes sense, before I close on it. Some of them are absolutely opposed to wholesaling. Some are more open to it. None of them like the fact I compete directly with them by trying to get owners to sell me their home with no agent. I've been attacked online and in the local media by agents who I have never even met, for the fact I try to buy homes direct from sellers. Invariably, they accuse me of trying to take advantage of people.

The truth is, many of them have bought my off-market deals themselves. They just don't like the competition! If you are a real estate investor, you'd better develop good relationships with at least a few agents.

Here are three main areas where I would use agents: market knowledge, help finding deals (pocket listings), and help finding buyers for your wholesale deals. And, of course, listing a property if you put it on the market. But that's something any agent will do, and is hardly adding value.

As for getting market knowledge: Agents have a world of information at their fingertips. They all have access to the MLS and all kinds of reports they can produce instantaneously. The main things you should be looking for: average prices in a submarket, DOM, number of properties pending versus active, average sales versus list price for the different submarkets which exist within every metro area.

Tomorrow morning, I could fly into a city I've never been to, and know absolutely nothing about, like Dallas, Texas. I'd head right over to a real estate brokerage, walk up to the receptionist, and say: "Hello, I am a real estate investor looking to buy some property here in town. Could I sit down with an agent?"

Then I'd tell the agent, "I came into some money that I would like to invest in real estate. I want to understand the market so I can do so wisely. Can you help me? Great, thank you. I'm trying to understand where some of the better areas are. I don't just mean as far as price, but also demand..." And then I would ask them for some of the information I just named.

This will tell me which parts of town are selling for $100,000 average in 79 DOM, versus the part of town selling for $250,000 average in 24 DOM, versus the part of town selling for $400,000 average in 128 DOM.

Let's say the price average for the entire Dallas market was $160,000 and the DOM was 68 on average (I just made these numbers up).

You'll notice the first example, $100,000/79 DOM, is both lower than the overall metro area's average price and higher DOM. That's two negatives. So that's my least favorite area. Would I still do a deal there? Hell yeah, but I would want more of a discount, since it's harder to sell, and with the lower dollar value, my upside won't be as much. The second example, $250,000/24 DOM, is a little more than 50% higher than the average price for the metro, and much lower for the DOM.

I like this submarket a lot. By the way, a submarket is how the agents divide the market, or it can be small towns. It's typically more than just a neighborhood, but less than an entire zip code. It might be 5,000 to 15,000 homes. Any bigger city or metro area will have dozens of submarkets.

The third example seems to be the luxury, high-end part of town. Prices are four times the first submarket we looked at and two and a half times the average for Dallas as a whole. The bad news is, like in many metro areas, it appears that homes on the luxury market are sitting for many weeks and months before selling. The DOM is almost double the metro average.

I wouldn't avoid this market, but though I like the prices (gives you more upside, and now buying a house 25% below means you get $100,000 in equity on average), the DOM is as significant in my mind, if not more so. Listen, there are one million dollar houses in every metro area in the country. Is a one million dollar home, though, really always worth the same to me, as an investor? In some markets, a one million dollar home is the epitome of high-end, and perfectly livable middle-class homes can be bought for $50,000.

There are way more luxury homes than wealthy people wanting to buy them, and that one million dollar home could sit on the market for a year or more before it sells. I know of someone who built an entire business around tying these up at huge discounts (Marco Kozlowski).

Other markets, like here in the San Francisco Bay Area, include dozens of neighborhoods where a home with an appraised or estimated value of one million dollars will sell in a single weekend, with multiple offers. Depending on its specific location/condition, they often fetch more than one million dollars.

As such, DOM can be the difference between strong demand and cashing out after one weekend, or waiting for a year to recoup your investment. As a wholesaler, it can mean the difference between success and complete failure. If demand isn't strong enough, you may have a hard time finding a buyer for your deal, even with a sizable discount. Again, you can still make money in all markets, but the weaker the market, the bigger the discount you will need and the pickier you should be.

If I had to choose, I would focus on the stronger DOM. The other stats I mentioned (pending versus active, and sales versus list price) will fill in the picture even more. If you see one house pending with 85 active listings, that means not many homes are going into contract, which is a sign of weakness. If there are 42 homes pending and only seven active, homes seem to be getting snatched up. Whether homes are selling at a discount or a premium from asking price can also tell you a bit about the direction of the market.

Talk to investors. These are the people who are going to be buying your deals if you're a wholesaler, so you'd better know what they want and what they think of the market. Go to REI (real estate investor) meetings. Every metro area has them; some have several. Some are good, some are weak, but what they all have in common—even the ones with bad presidents and weak speakers—is they attract investors. Network (try to come early, and prepare to stay late, as some clubs unfortunately don't allow time to get to know people *during* the actual meeting) and ask questions. Even if you're not planning to wholesale, it's very valuable to know how other investors are making money, especially the successful ones!

I've talked to many people at these meetings, the majority of whom aren't successful, full-time investors. They may be doctors or engineers who own a couple rental properties and have a couple buddies they like to hang out with once a month, or they may not own a single property yet, but trying to learn.

But then you'll also find someone who is actively fixing and flipping properties. That's the person you're looking for. Be nice to the others. Try to spend as much time talking to people who are actually actively buying and selling properties in that local market.

Unfortunately, they don't come with labels, so you'll have to just talk to a bunch of people until you find several like that (one is not enough). Get their information, and give them yours. This is where business cards would be useful, though I often don't have any on me. So do as I say, not as I do!

Read the blogs, get familiar with CoreLogic (corelogic.com), read your local newspaper's articles.

There's a lot of information online and in the local papers about what's happening in the real estate market. Take it with a grain of salt, as some people try to make themselves out like they can forecast the future, but do look for trends, especially if they are backed by statistics.

Whatever the market, know it, but realize, as I quoted my dad earlier, "there are always opportunities." It's your job to uncover them. They could be short sales in the lower-end parts of town, or luxury development projects in the higher-end areas. Or, as I have been doing in the last few years, both! This can and will change, so be nimble, and get ready to adjust your strategies every six to 12 months, based on what's happening. Probably, more like every 12 to 18 months, though it can happen sooner.

HOW TO GET STARTED RIGHT AWAY

1. Learn your market. It's crazy how many people don't even learn their market before trying to flip property. To me, it was obvious from the get-go, you need to know the prices and trends. I just talked about how to do this.

2. Find a deal. "But I don't have any money to market." I didn't either! I talked to agents and asked them what off-market fixer-uppers they knew about. Within a couple weeks, I landed my first one. If you *do* have money, there's more you can do.

But you must spend either the time or the money to do this. Don't tell me you have neither. Just choose which one to spend. I got my first two deals from agents. Made $25,000 and $20,000 on them. Then I started mailing to pre-foreclosures, and got really lucky (seriously, response rates on those are terrible, they're super-saturated). I wholesaled that one for $50,000.

Once you find a deal, get it under contract (e-mail me if you want a PDF copy of the California Association of Realtors form).

3. Find a buyer. Friends, friends of friends, acquaintances, businesspeople you know, Craigslist, REI meetings, property rolls, websites like Biggerpockets.com, and so on. There are lots of buyers out there for every market.

Oh yeah, and step 4: Get paid!

OTHER PEOPLE'S MONEY

A lot of people don't get involved in real estate investing because of the mistaken belief that it requires a lot of money. I used to believe this too, and it prevented me from getting involved in real estate until I was 34, especially because I lived in the most expensive housing market in the country. After all, how could I, who never had very high or stable income at that point, get involved in a business where millions change hands on a regular basis?

So my thinking went. You've probably heard the saying, "It takes money to make money." While that is sometimes true, here's the good news: It doesn't have to be *your* money!

Let's say you're as broke as a joke and you found a house for $700,000 that's worth $1 million. You have no money and not great credit. What are your options? Do you have to walk away from the deal? Absolutely not!

Here are some possibilities:

1. Get the house under contract and assigned (wholesale it).

2. Get a hard money loan for 70% to 75%. These are very common and easy to find, and are based on the asset value, not your financials. Credit and income don't really matter. For the other 25% to 30%, network with investors and offer them a certain percentage of the profit or a very high interest rate loan (they would be in second position after the hard money loan). For example, you may offer them 25% of the entire profit on the deal for putting up 25% of the money. Show them what a great deal this is. Or offer them a 15% interest rate secured by a deed of trust against the property. Remember that you may be broke, but there are billions of dollars out there looking for a good return. A billion sitting in a bank account earning 0% to 1% is not nearly as good of a deal.

3. Find a hard money lender who will lend up to 100%. Less common, but they're out there. Especially if you're buying a house worth $1 million for $700,000. Someone will probably lend you 100% of the purchase price. Think about it: They still have $300,000 worth of equity—essentially a "buffer" in case they have to foreclose. They might only get $750,000 or $800,000 for the house if they had to take it back, but that would still cover their loan.

4. JV, or joint venture. Find someone who will put up the money and then split the profit. 50/50, 60/40. Whatever. Make sure it's someone you trust and can get along with.

Friendships have been lost over business disagreements and deals gone sour. So put everything in writing and make sure everyone is clear on their role!

For example, when I did JVs with family members, either I was in charge of the project or someone else was, but never multiple people. That just tends to lead to conflict, as everyone has a different idea.

Where to find hard money lenders: real estate clubs, Facebook, and Google.

Where to find investors: real estate clubs (join them and network!), mailing lists of people who own multiple properties, mailing lists of cash buyers, talk to agents (some are investors too).

In my experience, there's more money looking for deals than there are deals. So be a deal finder and the money will come. You can become very wealthy using other people's money.

HOW TO FIND DEALS

Before we start, let me tell you that I try to avoid deals on the MLS. Why? A deal being on MLS means it has thousands of agents and all of their clients looking at it. If it's underpriced, whether as a strategy to get multiple offers or due to the agent's ignorance, the market will bid it up. If it's overpriced, it will probably still get some offers if it's at all desirable.

But most likely, it's an unreasonable, difficult seller who won't sell unless he gets his above market dream price, and a desperate enough agent (no shortage of those) who decided to take their listing anyway, because they're not too busy and it's worth a shot, and hopefully someday they will come to their senses, and I need a listing and beggars can't be choosers, and maybe he has friends who will list with me and I can meet potential buyers at the open house, and it gets my name and sign out there, blah blah blah.

Also, when a property is on MLS, many clients will feel you're ripping them off if you try to wholesale them something they could easily find themselves. At best, their level of excitement will be far less than if you say "I have an off-market deal." Everyone wants to know about the off-market deal. If you buy and put it back on the market, even if you do extensive work, everyone sees exactly what you paid for it.

Are there ever good deals on the MLS? Of course there are. I am sure there are investors who have made millions and *only* bought on the MLS. But there are so many advantages to finding off-market deals, and so many more of them, as a percentage, tend to be well-priced. I don't think there's any way I would have done anything close to my 35 deals in 2013–2014 if I had *only* scoured the MLS. I am sure I could have done a few. And they would, at least initially, have been met with a lack of enthusiasm on the part of buyers.

Okay, so how do you find good, off-market deals? That's the million-dollar question, right? Well, the multimillion dollar question, to be more accurate. There are so many ways. Pick three to five. Any less than three is putting too many eggs in one basket. More than five and you have diluted your efforts too much. Better to do a few things well than try to do too many and not do them well.

My three right now are: direct mail, pocket listings, and short sales (mainly through one agent who gets them for me, but occasionally others). I've always done the first two. I thought short sales would have dried up by now, but I just got one approved as I was writing this book, and I have a few more in the pipeline, so it looks like there will be at least a few more.

By the way, some banks are dumber (or less greedy, if you prefer) than others, and will let you get these short sales for way less than they're worth. I bought my own house as a short sale for hundreds of thousands below its value.

Ultimately, it depends on the bank (Wachovia [now Wells Fargo] loans were very easy to work with their short sale department) and on the negotiator on your end and on their end, and so forth. If and when short sales dry up, I will replace them with another method. I'm already going to be testing for a fourth method soon anyway. I was going to do Internet marketing—it seemed like the obvious choice—but some very successful investors told me it's basically a waste of money.

By the way, the Internet may not help you, but it can hurt you. I had some hate comments on there from agents and homeowners, many of them anonymous, and I know for a fact I lost some deals as a result.

It wasn't anything personal. I was out of the country once and I decided to send letters out with my friend Maria's name. We decided she would handle the calls and get some money out of any deals that we ended up closing. Anyway, we sent a few thousand letters with her name and number, and weeks later, she Google searches herself and finds a thread with all these mean comments about her. It happens when you market a lot as I do.

Many people will Google you on the Internet, but sellers looking online to actually sell their homes, if they do contact you, they are probably contacting a bunch of others; they are probably more sophisticated and trying to maximize every dollar out of their property. And that lead could still cost you as much as a direct mail lead. I'd rather have the direct mail lead.

Besides these four points just discussed, here are some more ways to find off-market deals:

- Probates (two ways to do this are by getting the list and contacting the executor, and also speaking to probate attorneys).
- At the auction or auction sites like auction.com, hubzu.com, genesisauctions.com, etc. (I am not including pre-foreclosure as a distinct category, because it falls under direct mail.)
- Telemarketing (but beware of the "do not call" list! major fines for violating).
- Networking with other attorneys and professionals, such as financial planners, CPAs, and others, who come in contact with owners who need to sell (this is one of those things I keep saying I should do, but never do).
- Bandit signs (didn't work for me and cops made me remove them, but others swear by them).
- Billboards (like bandit signs, but 100% legal and more credible; also expensive! Homevestors, with their "We Buy Ugly Houses" slogan, use them a lot; I am sure they work to some extent).
- Doorknockers (I love this. It works. Some people won't respond if you send them 1,000 letters, but when you're at their front door, they will open up. "Yeah, we are actually thinking about selling." I have gotten some great deals from these, including my $100,000 wholesale fee of 2015, but good luck finding anyone consistent and reliable to do this. It's very tough, many have flaked. If you figure out a good way, please let me know).

- Newspaper advertising (not many investors do this, but all the agents do; I've been told it builds your brand more than it generates calls. I want deals, not a brand, but may try it).
- Radio or TV advertising (another thing I haven't done, but thought about it).
- Buy leads (there are services; be careful, they usually suck. I may try again, but been burned).
- Visit garage and estate sales (sometimes these people are getting ready to sell the house).
- Get a list of city code violations.
- Craigslist (personally I hate that; too many eyeballs and BS/scammers/rookies; almost as bad as looking on the MLS for deals; but I'm sure it works once in a while).

WHY I THINK ONE HUNDRED LEADS A MONTH SHOULD BE THE GOAL

I have never kept an exact count (maybe I should) of how many leads I get and where they come from, but I am pretty sure that for the last two years, at least, I get about 100 leads a month, give or take 20. That sounds like a lot, but it's only three or four a day.

I get three or four leads a day pretty consistently, actually. About half of that is from my direct mail, and the other half from agents—pocket listings—and my bird-dog (a property scout who locates leads and passes them on to an investor, who then pays for the lead, usually when the deal closes), and once in a while, something else, like a referral from a friend or another investor giving me dibs.

The thing is, most leads are garbage. That's just the sad reality. If even 5% or 10% of leads were good ones, I could be making eight figures a year. But they're not. Between 98% to 99% are garbage. I can do something with 1.5% of the leads. So I do 1.5 leads a month, and have for the last two years.

That's of the 100 leads I look at. And four to six a year that I think are good enough to buy myself (six-figure profits). One hundred a month is what I look at, so that's 1,200 in a year. Meaning something between one in 200 or 300 calls or texts or e-mails I get about an off-market, supposedly good deal, materializes into a deal I figure is good enough to buy.

Now, if you're like the average investor, who is either a part-timer or a full-timer content with doing one or two deals a year, then you don't need to look at that many deals to make $50,000 or $100,000 a year—or maybe even $200,000 a year. But if you want to do this as a full-time business, you need to look at a lot of deals, because most of them won't make sense. This is true regardless of your market or what is happening. Why? Most agents just want to sell and make a commission. They won't scrutinize deals the way you do to make sure they make sense. It's not their money.

Well, when they get paid it is—it's their commission. But the money to buy the property is yours, not theirs. Their job is to make you buy a property. Your job is to treat your money with the respect and care it deserves, and to only use it to buy great deals with minimal risk, then to quickly make a profit and move on to the next deal. So, bottom line, even agents to whom you've explained what you're looking for will send you a lot of crap. The calls you get from sellers will be mostly from many who are unreasonable or unmotivated or not ready or talking to many others.

I can't tell you how many deals I've lost out on because some agent promised them an inflated number that I don't think even that very agent could get on the open market, and obviously I had no way to match.

Many sellers want more than the FMV (fair market value) of their house and aren't willing to sell for less.

Bottom line: there is no way around the fact you need to generate many leads to close a handful of good deals every year. I think 100 leads a month is a good number to shoot for. It's only three or four a day. That doesn't take very much time. I go see about 10% of these, if that. That's two or three houses a week, not a big deal. Most I can easily dismiss by looking at the comps as making no sense. If my source (agent, seller) still insists that they make sense, I am open to listening, but it's usually BS.

DIRECT MAIL

Let's talk about direct mail. I do a lot of direct mail. Unless you're completely broke, you should probably do some too. How many letters do I send? About 5,000 a month. I once told a friend—who is an agent—that I spend about $2,000 a month on direct mail (it's double or triple that now) and he said: "What? You're burning through $2,000 a month in letters."

Wow. What an idiot. "Burning through?" Those letters were making me 10 to 20 times what I spent on them. They still do, although some months it doesn't seem like it. And then, boom! You land a deal from a letter you mailed out six months ago. The three main ingredients in a direct mail campaign are the mail piece itself, the list, and the contents of your mail.

The contents of my letters are basically the main points I covered here in talking to sellers, which I emphasize in the letter. The letters themselves vary. I have a few friends who handwrite the names and addresses on the envelopes for me. They also stuff and seal the envelopes and put on the stamp. I pick up boxes of letters from them when they're done and drop them off at the post office, thousands at a time. I also use click2mail.com. I will soon try yellowletters.com and maybe another one. These are two of the biggest ones used by RE (real estate) investors. But like I said, there are many. They offer various postcards and types of letters.

Test and see what works best in your market. I didn't do well with postcards in the past. Close to zero response when I sent a few thousand. Maybe three or four phone calls, and nothing close to a good lead. Doesn't mean I will never try it again. You have to test and see what works. Maybe "I want to buy your house!" works better in some markets, or for some people, than a letter highlighting all the benefits of selling to me. You have to test, test, test. When you find what seems to work better, go with it, but keep testing occasionally.

Who to mail to? Here are some possibilities, and I have done almost all of these at one time or another. I tend to focus more on area, whereas most gurus tell you to focus on the seller's situation. So I might mail most people in a certain town or zip code. They will tell you to mail to those who are distressed or absentee owners. I will do that, too. It's good to mix it up. Here are some categories:

NODs (notice of default, or people in pre-foreclosure).
Absentee owners.
Free and clear owners.
High equity.
Negative equity (to try to get short sale deals).
By length of ownership.
Divorce.
Bankruptcy.
Probate.

Tax defaults.

By area (everyone in a certain neighborhood or zip code).

By property type (e.g., small, older house, a category with good upside potential).

Or a combination of these, such as an absentee owner who is getting divorced, or a free and clear owner of a small, old property, or someone who has owned a property for more than 10 years that has a lot of equity but hasn't been paying his taxes. Mix and match. You get it. There is no one right answer.

I keep mixing it up as well. I have a few areas I really like, though, and I keep mailing them. How often to mail to the same people? I would say three or four times a year is good. But if I try a new mailing list, and I get close to zero responses the first time, or just difficult people, I will probably drop that list or area and try a new one.

Depending where you live (for sure in California), you may be able to get leads for free from your title company. I do. Call up a title company that's local to you, and tell them you're an investor looking for leads. You will quickly find out if they provide that service or not. If not, try another one.

Apparently, in other parts of the country, it's less common than in California. There's a big company called CoreLogic with a service called ListSource that can get you leads of different demographics (sometimes ones the title company cannot) and all kinds of list brokers out there. There're also some shady ones, so beware.

OUTSOURCING

Here are some tasks I think can be outsourced, by level of difficulty.

Easy to outsource tasks:

E-mail writing (to agents, online leads, and so forth).

Scouring websites like Craigslist for leads or posting ads to find buyers.

Letter writing and stuffing.

Medium difficulty:

Talking to agents on the phone (you need actual interpersonal skills, and a solid command of the English language).

Talking to sellers on the phone (for example, answering calls and pre-screening them as they come in).

Analyzing deals (which requires more training and intelligence).

Extremely difficult:

Meeting with sellers to make an offer (I had never heard of anyone outsourcing this until a seminar I attended, but he didn't even explain how he did this).

Overseeing a rehab.

Meeting investors in person and being credible.

I have not outsourced any of these except the "easy" tasks, but I've been thinking of hiring someone to screen my calls. I may have to outsource more difficult tasks when I go live out of the country for a while. Or maybe I will just forget about doing any deals for that time period.

It definitely makes sense to outsource tasks like letter writing if you're making any kind of money or have time constraints. It's basically a $12- to $15-an-hour job, and your time should be worth more than that.

VIRTUAL AND LONG DISTANCE WHOLESALING

I haven't done this, exactly, but I did flip a few houses I never saw, and I did close a couple deals while I was traveling overseas. But I think what is meant by "virtual" is doing all your business online and by phone and never seeing the property or meeting the other people involved in this transaction.

I have met people who have done both these things, and I have read books. I met someone very impressive—who lives in New York City because he likes it there—who selected five markets in the country. For various economic reasons, he liked them, and he buys and sells and has agents and rehab crews in each of them. He visits each one a few times a year, but most of it he manages remotely.

DEALING WITH SELLERS

What do you tell sellers? My competition, for the most part, isn't really other investors. It's real estate agents. They have billion-dollar companies like Prudential and Coldwell Banker and RE/MAX behind them. There are millions of them, and they do a ton of marketing. All to convince sellers to list with them. And then comes little old me, saying, "Forget these agents. I'll buy your house. Don't put it on the market."

It really is David (me) versus Goliath. So why would they even consider selling to me (or you) when they have all these agents and the establishment telling them to sell through an agent?

Most won't sell to you, but here is how you can improve your odds: Tell them how easy it's gonna be. Make it sound much easier than dealing with an agent. And never be afraid to repeat yourself. Here are the main points in my marketing materials—and I also found out that some of the best in the business say very similar things, so I know I'm in good company, and that it works.

Key points you should make:

I will make you a very fair offer for your house.

I am not an agent. There is no commission.

Closing can be as long or short as you like.

I will buy your house in "as is" condition.

You will not pay any closing costs.

You can stay in the house for some time after selling.

If you have tenants, I will buy it with them.

If you're even thinking of selling some time in the next year, please call me.

HOW TO ACT IN FRONT OF SELLERS

It's generally good to meet sellers when you can. That is, when they're local. I try to make sure they are reasonable first. Without discussing price on the phone, if I can avoid it, I just ask if they're considering selling. If they say, "Everything is for sale for the right price," or, "No, I was just curious what you'd pay," I may not bother to go meet with them. If they say, "Probably not until next year," or, "Thinking about it, but haven't decided yet," that's probably as good as you're gonna get (90% of the time), and I go meet with them.

When people have already decided to sell, they often hire an agent. So, many times when they call me, they're just in the beginning of the process of considering selling. I want to build rapport with them *now*, before an agent or another investor does. I'm willing to invest five or six months in follow-up for a six-figure payday, and I have done this multiple times. But I am going to do that *only* when they sound reasonable (and sound like fairly nice people to do business with; I've never successfully bought a house from a total a-hole, as far as I can remember) *and* I think the property has a big upside. If it's not a great area or upside, I will still meet the seller if they seem reasonable, but I won't follow up as much afterwards. Maybe I should, but I won't. I will definitely make an offer though.

When the better properties (six-figure paydays) are not ready yet, I will be patient and won't make a written offer until they're ready to review one, which may be only after the third, fourth, or fifth meeting. Before that, we may speak in general terms about the price. There's usually a lot of small talk and rapport building that goes on. You may find yourself invited over for tea or even dinner.

I have to admit, I don't really like small talk. In fact, I don't consider myself a very socially outgoing person. But I have found it's important in establishing trust. I remember some guru I heard speak once said when you go to the seller's house, make comments about all their personal photos and little mementos. "Oh, is that your son? Did he play Little League? You like Hawaii, huh?" I dont know . . .

That's, again, blanket advice from the gurus that I think needs to be modified for the particular situation. I could see some people, who are all business, or just more reserved, really not liking that, especially when you've just met them for the first time when you showed up at their door. I don't think I would like it myself, if it's my first time having this stranger in my home.

Now, it's different when it's the second or third time you've met, and you're hopefully almost becoming friends. I know my friends can get away with saying things to me that would make me want to slap a stranger. Isn't that the same for everyone? You gotta build rapport.

How do you do that? Listen to them. Try to read what kind of person they are. It's not that hard, usually. Are they stern and serious, or do they make jokes? Do they smile a lot? Are they making small talk or asking questions about you? Adjust yourself accordingly. More or less mirror their behavior. I remember one house I got, by the third meeting our girlfriends met, and I was asking if I could have the Jack in the Box coupons that were hanging on his fridge. You think I would have done that with most sellers? Or during our first meeting? Hell no. You really need to adjust your behavior to the situation, and give some time for rapport to build. Trying to inject a little small talk, without getting too personal, is generally a good thing though.

I always come with a contract but I usually leave it in my car. Maybe 20% to 30% of the time, I end up writing the offer then and there. It depends if they're ready to sell at that moment. Like I said, most are not.

Here's a tip to help you close more deals: Offer a rent back, either free or discounted, if at all possible. It isn't always. But most sellers have lived in the home for decades. I deal with sellers who have been there for 30 years or more on a regular basis. Sixty years in one case. Often, they don't know where they will go next. They may know the area they want to move to, but need to find a home. Or they need the money to buy it. Or they're on the wait list for a retirement community.

Even *if* they know where they're going, and have it waiting for them, can you imagine moving after living 30 or 40 years in one house? It's going to take most people months to pack and move everything. So, if you can, offer a rent back. That way you can secure the deal, but they will still be living there after closing. Just be aware, it may make it harder to wholesale later, and if you're planning to rehab it or flip it, that's lost time during which your money is tied up and/or you're paying a mortgage. It's important to know your market, once again, if you do this.

I tried it in Berkeley, a famously liberal Bay Area city with strong rent control and tenant-friendly laws. After it worked in numerous other places, I failed to wholesale a property in Berkeley in large part because we put in the contract that the owners have a rent back. The buyers were familiar with Berkeley's infamous anti-landlord laws, and were afraid they'd be stuck with a deadbeat tenant (even though he didn't seem like that at all). I've done this in other cities and buyers didn't mind. It also depends what the plans are for the property.

Anyway, if it makes sense for you to offer, I can pretty much guarantee more sellers will say yes. So weigh the pain it is to you with the potential of getting the deal done.

POCKET LISTINGS: WHAT THEY ARE AND HOW TO GET THEM

In every market, you can use realtors to find below-market real estate deals. Most of these come in the form of "pocket listings."

What is a pocket listing? A pocket listing is a property listed with an agent, but not yet placed on a multiple listing service (MLS). In other words, it is not out there for the whole world to know about. Therefore, there is less competition, and a better chance of getting a bargain. Pocket listings are a big part of my lead mix.

How does it work? Usually, there is a time period between a week and a month, from the time an agent gets a listing until they advertise it and put it on the MLS. Before they do that, they need to prepare the house, clean it, stage it, promote it within the office, prepare flyers and signs, and so forth.

Most agents learn about these properties once in a while. It can either be their pocket listing, or it may belong to someone else in their office (or company, if they have multiple offices). If you network with enough agents, you will sometimes hear about pocket listings. You will often be the first to hear about deals, before they are widely advertised. Can you see the value in being the first to hear about a deal? Again, operating in a very competitive Bay Area market, I have picked up some great deals this way.

Here are the instructions for calling realtors to find pocket listings:

Get a list of local realtors from the Yellow Pages, ads, realtor.com, Google search, or any of a number of websites.

Many cities have more than 5,000 agents. Plenty to go around, and new ones all the time. Pick a place close to where you live or want to work. You will probably be surprised to see how many agents there are, even in small towns. Most of them have a phone number listed on their website.

Start calling them! If you call enough of them, some will have deals. When you call, this is what you should say:

"Hello, is this _____? Hi, my name is _____, and I am a real estate investor. I invest mostly in single family homes throughout _____ [name of area]. I buy and sell a number of homes each year. I usually try to add value, so I do fixer-uppers, and room additions, as well as tearing down old homes and building new ones. [Modify this based on your niche]. I have several contractors that I work with.

"I focus on properties that are not on the MLS. Do you have anything like that? Sometimes agents get pocket listings, or hear about them from a colleague. Do you get those sometimes? Can you call me when you do?

"I am very interested, and will pay a fair price. Do you know of anything right now that is not on the MLS?"

Pause! And wait for their response. Hopefully, at this point they say, "Well, as a matter of fact ..." or, "Um ... there might be. Let me check."

To which you should say: "Okay, please call me as soon as you hear of anything not on MLS. We also sell homes, and can provide you with listings, if you can help us find deals. Thank you!"

If they say they will have something soon, or sound like they really want to work with you, write down their name and number, and call them about a week later. Like most things, part of the system is follow-up. You have to keep reminding them that you are out there, looking for deals, so that when they do come across one, they will think of you first.

Many realtors will ask why you don't want to work with properties on the MLS. Tell them you've been investing for some time, and in your experience, the better deals are the ones that not everyone knows about. Since the MLS is accessible by anyone, you could search it yourself, but need their help identifying deals that are not yet widely known. It is a reasonable question, but if, after you have answered it, they still insist you should work with the MLS, or try to tell you it's impossible to find deals not on the MLS, then they are not someone you can work with. Thank them for their time, and move on to the next agent.

Remember: You can call more than one agent at the same company, but *not* within the same office. This will only backfire, as sooner or later they will find out, and it will be awkward (and possibly against their office rules) for them to be working with the same client as the guy two cubicles away.

This is a great way to find deals, but a word of caution: Not every realtor wants to work this way. Most of them are used to doing things the easy and conventional way—clicking a few buttons to look up properties on the MLS. They will either tell you they will call you, but they are not really interested, or they will tell you up front. I prefer the ones who tell me up front that they won't work this way, as it saves me follow-up time.

In my experience, roughly one out of seven realtors will try to find deals this way. So call seven. No, call 70! If you call 70, and follow up (I can't emphasize this enough), you will have 10 realtors calling you with pocket listings.

By the way, when I say they will call you, it doesn't mean you will hear from them every week or even every month. The other day, I made an offer on a house. This was a pocket listing. The agent who brought me the deal was someone I had met once, and had not heard from in five or six months. I didn't think they were serious, so I stopped following up. It took me a while to even remember meeting this person. I forgot about him, and I figured he forgot about me. But he had not. He remembered that I was looking for pocket listings, and when he found one, he immediately thought of me and called.

There is an important principle here: Put the word out there, to enough people, that you are looking for deals, and deals will come your way. Happy hunting!

REAL CASE STUDIES

I did 18 deals in 2014. All different kinds. I made from $10,000 to $450,000 on deals, and I kept a couple as rentals. Here are a few case studies of different types of deals I have done:

1: **"Deal of the century."** Double close on a high-end deal. Net profit: $450,000, with no work done to the property whatsoever. Bought and sold off market. Let's also talk about what double closing is, how it works, and why I feel it is way underused and underrated when we discuss this deal. Deal source: Direct mail.

2: **"The mistake."** Got a property under contract from Julie, an agent I had met through my VA (virtual assistant). Looked decent from the comps, but very nice in person. Needed very little work and had great views. Decided to wholesale it to a friend. Got paid $10,000. He and his partner made $140,000, doing almost nothing to the house. My mistake? Wholesaling when I should have bought it. Deal source: Pocket listing.

3: **"The biggest wholesale deal."** Got a property as a teardown in a high-end area. Meaning a new, luxury home will be built there by the developer. I think my contract price was $1.7 million. I wholesaled it for $100,000. This is the most I ever made on a wholesale deal. Deal source: Doorknocker.

4: **"Where's that?"** I have a bird-dog out of state who sends me stuff he finds online. I only pay him when he brings me a deal I end up buying, and frankly, most of them are crap. This was the third deal he found me in about two years. He sends me leads almost every day, but I often don't like them. Anyway, he connected me with an agent who had a property in a place called Bay Point. I wasn't even sure where that was, but then I remembered seeing the name on the BART (Bay Area Rapid Transit) map. It's the last stop.

What intrigued me was this was a four-bedroom, two-bath house for $130,000 in the Bay Area. That's the kind of price you'd expect in the

Midwest or South. It was on the outskirts, and not the best area, but it was 35 to 40 minutes by car or BART from San Francisco, where a one-bedroom apartment is usually close to $1 million. And here's this four-bedroom *house* for $130,000.

I immediately thought I could keep this as a rental, checked around, and asked my property manager. He said it should rent for $1,500 a month or a bit more. That definitely worked with my 10% rule (annual rents equaling 10% or more of purchase price + fix-up costs). The place was a dump, and as I write this, my contractor is nearly done with it. The repairs and remodel are costing me $30,000. So the house cost me $160,000 with that, and should rent for $1,500 a month, and is worth $200,000 to $220,000 based on comps and what I have even been offered verbally. Good deal to buy and hold. Deal source: Pocket listing via my bird-dog.

5: **"Rehab."** Got a short sale in a not-so-great part of San Jose. Needed work and I hired a contractor and put about $30,000 into it. Put it back on the market and it sold fast. Made about $70,000. Deal source: Short sale via agent.

6: **"Duplex."** Got a duplex via short sale for $420,000. Used cash from deal 1 to buy all cash. Spent $50,000 to remodel it and add a bedroom to the back unit. Both units are now two-bedroom. Rents for $4,000 a month. Source: Short sale via agent.

These are a few examples. As you can see, the source of the deal, the price ranges, the submarket it was in, as well as the strategy of how it was structured were all different. Direct mail, pocket listings, bird-dogs, and short sales were all employed to get the deal. Wholesaling, rehabbing, double closing, and keeping as a rental were all exit strategies.

If I had limited myself to just wholesaling or to just rehabbing or to any one strategy, I would have made a fraction of the money. If I could not close some of these in my name, with me as an owner (even if just for a few weeks in some cases), I would have made a fraction of the money. If I had only used direct mail as a marketing strategy, I would have made a fraction of the money. If I had only used pocket listings, I would have made a fraction of the money.

You get it, right? Do multiple things to get deals. Then structure them in the most profitable way, taking into account risk and the value of your time ($120,000 is more profit than $80,000, but I will take $80,000 today as a wholesale fee rather than rehab and hopefully make $120,000 three months from now. So it's not always just profit—time and risk also need to be accounted for).

ANATOMY OF A DEAL

Here are two examples of how a deal goes down:

Example 1: Pocket listing

Monika forwards me an e-mail from Julie, an agent who says she has an off-market deal. I call Julie and she gives me the address. I run the numbers and the deal looks okay, but not great. Maybe $50,000 below market on a $950,000 house. It's in a high-end area, but one with a price ceiling that isn't that much more than this property. The property has limited development potential. There isn't a possibility to tear it down and build a new house and make a bunch of money. In some Bay Area communities, that is possible, so this is an important distinction. Although it's a good neighborhood, it's not the most coveted in the area, and there isn't much upside. I meet with Julie and she is very pleasant. I decide I will probably wholesale this property. I call and text a few other people I know.

One of them, we'll call him Pete, is an agent who works and lives in this area. He seems very interested. In addition to being an agent, Pete is also an investor and sometimes buys my deals direct. None of my other investors seem interested, and I am not surprised. It's a good area but, again, not the best one, and there doesn't seem to be much upside. I go to see the house with Pete, and it looks very good and needs minimal work. Nevertheless, based on the comps and my investors' lack of interest, I am more certain than ever that I will just wholesale this deal.

Julie thinks it's a very good deal, but agents usually tell you that, so I take it with a grain of salt. Sorry, Julie! (She is reading this section). I notice in comps that *bigger* houses sold for $100,000 to $200,000 more. I don't see enough profit here to use almost $1 million of my own money. I am very cautious and need to be sure.

I ask Julie to write up the offer, making sure she makes the contract assignable (this can be done in one of two ways: either you put "and/ or assignee" after your name as the buyer or, under other terms and conditions, write or have the agent write "buyer may add partner or assign contract"). Our offer is accepted, and I now have a deal I can either close on or wholesale. I wholesale the deal to Pete for $10,000. Why so cheap? Nobody else wants it, and he says it's a skinny deal. Would he have paid more? Probably a little bit. I don't think he was that sure about it, either. Pete partners with another agent, they do almost nothing to the property, and end up making about $140,000. My mistake? You bet. I could have made more, but lack of enthusiasm from investors and comps looked marginal, so I wholesaled, and made very little. Sometimes it's better to err on the side of caution.

Example 2: Larchwood

One of my bird-dogs wants to be a real estate investor and he basically wholesaled me a deal. He started mailing to absentee owners and found a willing seller who lives out of town. We meet at the property in San Jose, which comps in the mid-$700,000s after remodel. The sellers believe it needs $100,000 of work and would rather not deal with it. The house does need a lot of work, but I am sure I can get it done much cheaper. They want $620,000 or $630,000 (I can't remember). I leave them with an offer for $600,000 on the CAR form (California Association of Realtors real estate purchase contract) after we talk with them for a while at the house (it was a rental, now vacant).

I emphasize to them how easy this will be for them, the fact they are paying no commission or closing costs (remember, I always pay the closing costs when I buy direct from an owner—a fairly low cost to me, and high perceived value to them; but not normally when there's an agent involved) and that the house does need a lot of work. So on one hand, I am emphasizing the ease of working with me, and then I am telling them how much work the house needs. I really don't think I would have paid much more than the $600,000. The seller calls me the next day and says he will accept my offer. I say great and thank you. Before I open escrow, I shoot it over to a couple investors. They are very interested. I know I am getting a very good deal.

The worst comps, on a busy street nearby, sold in the high $600,000s. Most are all over the $700,000s and into the low $800,000s. I agree with Mark to pay him 20% of the profit. I remodel the house for about $35,000, stage and list with an agent. It sells for $770,000 after two open houses, and we make $90,000 in profit.

By the way, note that about half the spread between the sales price ($770,000) and purchase price ($600,000) was expenses, not profit. And this with a relatively inexpensive rehab. Commission and various carrying costs like taxes and closing costs (twice—once when I bought, and again when I sold) ate up the rest. That's why we need a good discount when we buy a property! You probably need at least a 10% discount off FMV just to break even! Rookies confuse the spread between the potential sales price and the purchase price as profit, and many agents who should know better talk that way too.

Here's a twist: Right after I closed, before remodeling and putting it on the market, I had told a couple agents about it. One of them had a buyer who submitted an offer for $730,000 on it as is. They didn't want me to remodel. I would have made $100,000 on that deal, slightly more than I ended up making after remodeling and listing it. Remember this when we discuss double closing and why I think rehabbing is overrated and double closing is underrated.

Random story: I met with a real estate buddy for coffee a few months ago. Nice lady, but we don't see each other often, as we live in different parts of the Bay. She was too busy telling me about her drama to ask me any questions or what I have been up to. Anyway, her drama was that she'd just rehabbed a house two hours from where she lives (the total opposite end of the Greater San Francisco Bay Area region). She was going there several times a week, and the rehab took nine months. The contractors were a nightmare. In fact, she was suing them (you know who wins in a lawsuit? Hint: They went to law school). Blah blah blah. I no longer remember all the details. At the end of this lengthy and nightmarish process, she made about $140,000. If she had taken the time to ask me anything, I would have told her about my deal (which is actually located a mere five miles from where she lives). It was a pocket listing I ended up rehabbing. It took me three weeks and I made almost the exact same amount as my dramatic friend: $140,000.

Every rehab I have done so far has taken about three weeks. Every one so far has cost about $30,000 to $35,000. I gotta be honest: I don't do the most high-end rehabs, generally. No one walks in and says, "Wow! This house should be in a magazine!" But I don't spend a fortune or a lot of time. I like to flip quickly. Unless you are doing an addition, it really shouldn't take that long or cost that much. You could also over-improve a property and then it's not the best way to spend your money or time. Time is money. During the nine months my friend was anguishing over her one rehab, I probably did more than a dozen deals. Not to mention the stress of having all your money tied up for so long. I've done that with new construction, but the payoff is usually $1 million or more on those (split among partners).

EVALUATING DEALS

How do I check if a deal is a good deal? First is my own general market knowledge, which comes from doing deals and watching prices and trends in the area. This market knowledge is essential and a step many beginning wholesalers neglect. They focus on marketing or finding buyers when their first step should be understanding their market.

Then there are four ways. I rely on these particularly in areas or types of properties I'm less familiar with:

1. Feedback from realtors

If realtors I respect tell me it is (or isn't) a good deal, I take that into account. Although they can be wrong or have their own agenda (to get the listing), so it's only one factor.

2. Interest from investors

If investors are interested and willing to pay more than I can get the property for, that is a very significant factor. Money talks, and I should be able to make money on it. Normally, that means the market value is even higher.

3. Craigslist ads

Put a "ghost ad" on Craigslist. I don't normally give exact address, but street and general size, condition, and so on. I make the price 10% to 20% higher than I'm getting it for. If I get 10 or more real replies (not agents wanting to list it or other wholesalers/lowballers), that is encouraging. Few or no real replies is a cause for concern.

Before I bought my condo for $200,000, I got about 15 replies when I advertised it for $245,000. This helped convince me to buy it. I sold it two months later for $320,000.

4. Comps

Pretty obvious that you study what similar properties have been selling for. Though in a rapidly changing market, even two-month-old data can be outdated.

It's important to look at *sold*, not so much at active or pending comps. After all, anyone can list a property for any price. What someone is actually willing to pay is all that matters.

A fifth component is understanding the property's attributes and the market itself.

A very "unique" property may be difficult to sell. A property with better schools than those surrounding it can sell for much more. I've been both helped and hurt by these things.

The second item is usually the most important for me. Since I'm still wholesaling the majority of my deals, I need an investor who wants it. And even if I were to buy it myself, it means a lot to me. But with the "$150,000 mistake" deal, there was very little interest from investors. I never tried Craigslist ads on it, but the feedback from realtors was that it was a good deal, and the comps showed it was a good deal (though not as high as it went). Understanding the fifth component—the market being very hot, and giving more weight to it having very good schools—should have made it clearer this was a very good deal.

I don't always have to go through all of these. Sometimes I just know, and sometimes the comps are there and the interest is weak, or the comps aren't great but the interest is strong. Of course, I am always learning myself through doing deals or when deals don't work out.

But these are good tools to have at your disposal.

STRUCTURING DEALS

I've talked about evaluating deals. Now let's talk about structuring them for maximum profit. It's largely in structuring the deals that I went from six figures to seven figures in this business. Think about it—even if you're the best wholesaler around, you're limited in your income. With extremely rare exceptions, your checks will range from a few thousand to a few tens of thousands. Nothing wrong with that, unless you can do better.

At one point it hit me: To build real wealth, I needed six-figure checks, not five-figure checks on a regular basis. The difference between making $200,000 to $300,000 a year to $1 million-plus is the difference between making a living (a good living, albeit, but still just making a living) and building wealth.

I don't know about you, but I would rather build wealth than just make a living. Looking back now, I've left so much money on the table when I was just wholesaling, it makes me want to cry. I left behind millions. I would wholesale a high-end property for $25,000, and they would rehab it and sell it for $300,000 to $500,000 profit. This happened many times. I could not have done all of these deals, perhaps, but I could have cherry-picked a few.

And this is basically what I do now. I cherry-pick. I do the best ones myself, and wholesale the rest. Sometimes, I get it wrong, and I end up wholesaling one I should have kept. But I am pretty conservative and cautious (look at the title of this section; minimizing risk is huge to me) so it hasn't happened yet that I bought something I shouldn't have. I look at more than a thousand deals a year and pull the trigger just a few select times.

There are a couple of different kinds of deals. Basically two categories, I guess. I'm not counting the 98% of deals you are passing on because they make no sense. Although, some of those could maybe fit into the first category.

CATEGORY 1: DEALS THAT SHOULD BE WHOLESALED

You've run the numbers, you've done your homework, and there is just hardly any margin to make them work. Only a retail buyer would want this property. There's not enough discount from FMV (fair market value), there isn't the possibility to improve it substantially and make a lot of money. It just doesn't make sense. But you think you can maybe find a retail buyer for it. In this case, you call agents who have retail buyers, or maybe you have a list of retail buyers yourself.

I've never dealt with retail buyers myself, for reasons that may be obvious, but I will gladly explain: Basically, they're a pain in the ass to deal with, need a lot of hand-holding, are not repeat customers, are very fickle (the husband likes it, the wife doesn't; "we changed our mind, we want a bigger kitchen," and so on) and are used to working with agents anyway. They also don't get wholesaling, and think it's some kind of scam. ("Wait, who are you? You're not the owner? You're not an agent? You want to sell me a contract?")

I have successfully wholesaled to many retail end users, but not directly—through someone they trust. Either their agent, who assures them it's legit, or they're friends with one of my investors, who assures them it's legit.

I guess part of the reason I am not an agent is that I wouldn't have the patience to deal with most customers. The property is maybe 5% below market, but that could be enough for you and an agent to both get paid. You get your assignment fee from the retail buyer and split it with the agent. You never deal directly with the buyer, their agent does (they need to be okay with the wholesaling concept and explain it to their buyer; many won't, but some will).

CATEGORY 2: EVERYTHING ELSE

These deals have some real upside that you can see. They range from an okay deal to the "deal of the century." Personally, my basic rule is very simple: I won't buy it if I can't make at least $100,000 on it. Normally, that is. If it's a $200,000 condo, and I think I can make $50,000 net just double closing on it, I will do that. Much less effort, so that's acceptable. Also, like the house I bought a couple months ago for $130,000 in Bay Point, if it makes sense as a rental.

Otherwise, I don't want to use my money and potentially borrow money to buy a property if I can't flip it and net at least $100,000. I do maybe four to six like this every year and wholesale everything else. Sometimes I miscalculate and make $80,000 or $90,000 instead of $100,000 or more. Sometimes I also end up making $100,000 more than I thought. I'm in and out real quick, whether I am rehabbing or double closing. The only exception is new construction. I haven't really done additions yet, except to my own house and duplex.

So how do I decide when to "pull the trigger" and what to do? To wholesale, or buy myself, or partner with someone or what?

First, I put out some feelers to see what the demand is like. If I have a property under contract, I ask people if they are interested at a price some number higher than my contract price. Let's say I'm in contract for $500,000. I might tell people there's this deal they can have for $550,000, and see how interested they are. If everyone is interested, and the comps and everything else is positive, there's a good chance I will do it myself.

Do my buyers get pissed? Not really, because these are people I do a lot of deals with and they know I'm sometimes going to buy it myself. Frequently, I've only texted them and they did a bit of research, or know the area.

Here's an example of the very first property I bought all by myself a few years ago, and how it happened: After months of waiting, I got a short sale approval for a condo for $200,000. This was a referral from a friend. The seller was another friend of hers. The Bay Area market was in an upswing. I mentioned it to an agent friend, and he said he thought he could get someone who would buy it for $230,000 or $235,000. So I would get about a $15,000 wholesale fee on it.

For some reason, that didn't seem like too good of a deal for me. The price was low enough that I could come up with my own cash to buy it. I had been waiting for months for it. It was completely remodeled and in a good area. It didn't feel right to only make $15,000 on it. I was still renting myself at this time, not yet a homeowner. As I said, it was the very first property I bought myself. So I considered moving there, but although I liked the area, it was pretty far from the part of the Bay Area that I was used to living in and doing most of my business in. Anyway,

I was pretty sure I was going to close myself, and figure out what to do later.

This brings up another point. When you get a great deal, you don't have to know at the time what exactly you are going to do with it.

If someone were to sell me a Ferrari right now for $10,000, assuming it's not stolen, I would buy it in an instant. I know the car is worth so much more. I will buy it, but I am not sure if I will just resell it or drive it myself. And I don't need to decide when I buy it. Earlier, I discussed a property that was my first JV, non-wholesale deal. My family ended up remodeling and putting it on the market and we made $400,000 net profit. What I did not mention was after we bought it, there was a vigorous debate (to put it mildly) between my brother, on the one hand, who felt very strongly that we should do a big addition to it (it was a small, three-bed, one-bath house, on a large one-third acre lot in a high-end area, so his argument did make sense) and my parents, who just wanted to remodel.

There was even brief talk of scrapping it and building a brand new house. So we bought a property without even knowing what we would do with it. Why? Because it was a great deal. In the end, my parents won the argument (I largely abstained, but sided with them, mainly because I wanted and needed the money sooner rather than later) and we remodeled the house.

It took three weeks and cost $50,000. It sold after one weekend on the market, and the profit was $400,000. By the way, our buyers *did* end up building a new house and living there for a couple years before listing it recently for $3.895 million.

Once again, I got sidetracked. Back to my condo.

I was getting it for $200,000. There were a few good signs: My agent friend said he could find someone to buy it for $230,000 to $235,000.

The comps seemed to show it was worth in the mid-$200,000s. I called a couple local agents and they also said mid-$200,000s. All this, plus it was remodeled and in a good area. That might have been enough, but it was the first property I was about to buy and close on myself, with no partners, and with my own money. Even $200,000 seemed scary back then with my own money!

So, this was probably overkill, but I decided to put an ad on Craigslist. I took a couple photos, gave the size and condition (remodeled) and I gave the street name, but not the specific address in the ad (you usually shouldn't; you never know who's reading this. Craigslist is filled with phonies, weirdos, and scammers; and until you close on a deal, it can backfire, as it usually gets back to the owner. Ask me how I know!). I listed it at $245,000.

When I got about 20 replies, most of them seeming very legit (not a Nigerian prince wanting to send me a cashier's check!), I was convinced, along with all the other evidence, that I would buy this one.

I did, and then I decided to rent it out. My property manager, who was also a broker, prepared the rental listing and started showing it to people. Then we found that it could not be rented. The condo HOA had a restriction where only six out of the 36 units could be rented out, and there was already a waiting list to rent more.

Apparently, I had never read the HOA docs as I should have. Another reason I don't really want to own condos long-term. You are at the mercy of the HOA. Anyway, I decided to sell it. This was about a month after I bought it for $200,000, and no work at all was done to it or needed. It sold with multiple offers for $320,000, all cash. There was actually a $5,000 higher offer, but my broker wisely urged me to take the all-cash offer, because in the fast rising market we were in, it might not appraise and then the non-cash buyer would have problems with the loan.

Anyway, I cleared about $100,000 in profit. That's more than a 50% return on my cash in less than two months. I sure am glad I didn't wholesale it for $15,000 to my friend's client. It also gave me a big confidence boost in buying and closing on a property, and reinforced I was leaving a lot of money on the table by just wholesaling. It took me to the next level psychologically.

There is no 100% hard-and-fast rule on when to wholesale versus buy a property. I would rather wholesale for $70,000 then try to make $100,000. But if it looks like I can make $100,000, I don't want to wholesale for $15,000 either. It also depends on the price range, of course.

A $100,000 profit on a $1 million property is not as impressive as making $100,000 on a $200,000 condo, and there's a lot more risk. Just keep one thing in mind: It is very difficult and unlikely that you will buy more than four to six properties a year that you actually close on. Four to six.

I know several very successful investors who do more or less what I do, with or without the wholesaling part, and they're all in this range as well. They close on four to six properties a year. I think that's because you don't find that many good deals, even if *you're* good, and each one takes some time. So, I want to cherry-pick those. I want six-figure profits. I want minimum risk. Otherwise, I want a wholesale fee.

HOW TO DETERMINE YOUR WHOLESALE FEE

This is more of an art than a science. It's supply and demand. I refuse to make less than $10,000. I rarely ask for more than $50,000. This is probably not good, but as I have made more in my business in general, my average wholesale fees have actually gone down. I think for two reasons: I am keeping many of the juicier ones that would have resulted in bigger wholesale fees and wholesaling is no longer my main source of income, more of a secondary byproduct (it constitutes 75% of my deals, but only 25% of my income), so I don't push as hard on the fee.

In general, and this is an extreme overgeneralization, you should probably make about 5% of your property sales price as a wholesale fee on average. So if you are selling the property for $400,000, that's $20,000. Obviously, it depends how good the deal is. That's why this is a rough average, and as I said, I am overgeneralizing. But the thing is, most buyers and investors—if you are a wholesaler—almost see you as taking the place of an agent, and look to pay you about the amount they normally pay an agent, which is 5% or 6% (total commission). How to determine your *exact* wholesale fee: I don't know, and I've done hundreds of wholesale deals. Send me an e-mail if you figure it out!

PARTNERSHIPS

Another way to structure deals is with partnerships. I will say that I would only do this with people I really trust. I've done it mostly with family members, and a few trusted individuals. Another point is someone needs to be in charge. Make sure your partner is okay with that, if it's you, or you are okay with that if it's your partner. Many times, one of the people is a largely "silent partner" who is just investing their money, while the other is investing his or her time and effort (and may or may not invest money as well).

There are ways to structure deals where instead of getting a wholesale fee upfront, you get paid on the back end, or possibly some combination. I generally partner only on some of the bigger and lengthier deals, and always (so far) on new construction projects, which take 12 to 18 months and typically cost about $2 million or more.

RENTAL PROPERTIES

Being a landlord is a pretty new experience for me, but I own a few rental properties now, and it's been nice to see the money come in every month. I don't have a mortgage on them, so the expenses are minimal, although I spent a considerable amount of money upfront remodeling them, and in one case of a duplex, adding a bedroom. Here are my personal principles on buying rental properties. And, as I am new to this field of being a landlord, I reserve the right to change my mind. But I think this makes some sense:

1. As with any real estate, I don't want to buy a rental property unless it is a good deal. The rentals I have bought have all been at least 20% to 30% below market value.

2. Unlike with my flips, I *am* open to buying rentals on MLS. Since I don't need to convince someone else that it was a good deal and get them to pay more than my contract price, what do I care? If the numbers on a rental make sense (see 4 below), I will buy it. *However*, in the competitive Bay Area, the numbers won't usually work unless it is off market.

3. I don't want to own rentals in the crappiest areas. Returns are better on paper, but it also means more headaches and problem tenants.

4. I look for gross annual rents to be about 10% of the purchase price. For example, if I buy a house for $360,000, I want rents to be $36,000 a year, or $3,000 a month. If it's a condo (none so

far), and there is HOA, that should be deducted from the rents to arrive at this figure. So, $1,500 a month rent, but $300 a month HOA, is really only $1,200 a month rent.

5. I want to own rentals within an hour drive of where I live. So, basically, right now only in the Bay Area. These are also properties that I can easily sell for a nice profit should I choose to do so. These are markets I know and understand, and are strong markets. Note: I have decided, after I reach my income goals with local rentals (I'm a fourplex away now), I am going to be considering out-of-area rental properties and other real estate investments. For now, I am keeping it local.

6. I like having a property management company. My whole philosophy and goal in my business is to build a lifestyle business, where I have residual, passive income and am free to do what I want, when I want, and go where I want. Screening tenants and fixing toilets does not fit into that program. I pay my property manager 7% of the rents I receive.

MISTAKES

"Do as I say, not as I do."

Because I'm far from perfect, as a human being and as a real estate investor, here are some things I *should* do, but don't:

1. Do try to get MLS access

I have managed without it, using the online tools like Redfin, Trulia, Zillow, et cetera, and also getting comps and feedback from agents. I feel confident using these tools combined with a decent knowledge of most submarkets where I operate to determine if a deal is good or not. I could fairly easily get MLS access, and I should, but never have. But you should, it helps. I'm sure I sometimes miss things I should know because I don't have it. You need an agent friend to get access.

2. Do ask sellers if they're open to carrying back a mortgage

I've almost never done this. Some build their whole business on it. I don't think it works often in high-end areas, but some sellers will say yes, and it lets you structure deals differently when you do. Less money down, better terms, potential to do more deals, and so on. It has advantages. I just don't really use it. But I should, and you should. It doesn't hurt to ask.

3. Do be organized, especially with your leads and contacts and tracking your results

I'm embarrassed to say it, but I have lost good leads that I wrote down on a little scrap of paper or the edge of a newspaper when the call came in, and forgot to write down somewhere else. I'm also not very methodical about tracking down which calls come from which mailing. I can't tell you how many calls/leads I got from my latest mailing campaign where I spent more than $6,000 or what my exact response rate was overall.

I've been going more with my gut feeling and general sense of what seems to be working, without really compiling and studying the figures. In a way, my philosophy is, "Throw enough shit against the wall, and some of it will stick." In other words, I know if I do enough marketing and networking, the leads will come and keep on coming. But if I were to analyze things better, I am sure I could improve my marketing results. So don't be like me. Be organized in general and track your results.

4. Follow up regularly with all leads

This is embarrassing. I've let good leads slip through the cracks, didn't follow up enough, and they ended up selling to someone else or listing on the open market. I do try to follow up but this is tied to my poor organization skills. I write my leads down in a notebook or on my iPhone's notes app. I am trying to get better at this. Many of my best deals, including the ones I got directly from sellers and made six figures on, required months of following up. So it's not like I never do this. It's just I could improve in this area. Most deals, especially the good ones, are made in the follow-up.

So, I admit I'm not very good at these things, and some of them are pretty important. But this should be encouraging to you, because in spite of it, I am still successful. Why? Because I have gotten good at the three steps of house flipping: generating many leads, evaluating them, and structuring them for maximum profit. I know my market, and I have networked with agents and investors. And, when I have a hot prospect in front of me, I am very tenacious.

LIES AND TRUTHS

Let me be clear: Almost everyone who has written a book or teaches a class on real estate has some good knowledge and wisdom to impart. I have learned something from almost everyone I have read or listened to. Nevertheless, I have also read and listened to enough real estate gurus to see that most of them spout a lot of the same BS. A few of these things really irk me, because you hear them repeated so often. They make them sound like absolute rules, which they are not, and what bothers me is a lot of newbies in the business follow them, and shoot themselves in the foot. It causes them to either spend a lot of time doing the wrong things, or miss opportunities. Let's explore these fake "rules," which I am going so far as to call "lies," and replace them with the truth.

Lie 1: Build a big buyers list

Truth: The only people I know who spend a lot of time building big buyers lists are rookies. This business is about relationships, not lists. You need a few key relationships. A few investors, a few agents, and that's all you need. If you're dealing with real and competent investors and agents, and you got a good deal, you will find a buyer this way. If you don't, either it's not a good deal or you don't have the right investors/agents.

It is very easy to build a "buyers list." I can tell you right now how to get dozens or possibly hundreds of potential "buyers" within a day. Place an ad for a below-market property in a highly desirable area on Craigslist. You will get a lot of responses. Guess what? A lot of them will be wholesalers, rookies, wannabes, scammers, and so on. Find real investors and agents, don't just build some meaningless list. It's about having a few strategic relationships. With those in place, you put together deals.

Lie 2: Offer a max of 70% of ARV (After Repair Value of the property) minus the cost of repairs

Truth: It is foolish to use this absolute rule and not vary from it. However, I have known at least one successful investor who followed this formula. I had a lot of respect for him, so a few years ago, I invited him to see a property we were rehabbing (I bought this one with family members; this was in 2010 and was actually the first deal I didn't "wholesale"). It was in a high-end Silicon Valley neighborhood, where prices were on the way up and demand was strong. There was absolutely nothing lower than the low $1 millions. I brought my friend to see the house, which we had recently bought and were rehabbing. I told him we paid $875,000. I showed him the comps, the same ones I looked at. He said, "I wouldn't have paid more than $770,000 for this house." Three weeks later, we sold this house for a $400,000 *net* profit, after a $50,000 rehab.

I can tell you with absolute certainty, the seller would not have taken one dollar less than $875,000 (I know, because I tried!). A few months later, my friend passed up on another great deal I brought to him. Someone else bought it and made a lot of money. His lowball approach has certainly gotten him some good deals—some great deals—but he has also missed out on many opportunities, some worth six figures, by being inflexible. I refer to most of my fellow real estate investors affectionately as "bottom-feeding lowballers."

This does not apply to the developers and sophisticated investors I network with. But most investors seem to think the only way to make a buck in real estate is to buy a house at a steep discount from a "motivated seller" (see lie #4). By doing this, they miss out on many great opportunities. The biggest problem with this formula is it doesn't take into account where your market is physically located and where in the market cycle it is.

Would you really not adjust your offer based on whether the market was rising or declining? Based on whether you're in a sub-market, like some small towns in the Bay Area for example, where there are many more buyers than homes on the market, and homes get dozens of offers if they go on MLS? Or whether the homes are sitting for months on the market without selling? What about the potential for the property to be improved? Some properties you can add half a million dollars in value, like a small house on a big lot in a high-end area.

Other properties (like a remodeled condo) you can't do anything to add value to. There are houses I would gladly buy at 5% to 10% off FMV of their as-is condition, and others I wouldn't touch for less than 50% off. It depends on all these factors. Of course, when you're teaching rookies, it's easier to oversimplify things, and of course, this simplistic 70% formula *can* work, but it often misses the mark.

Lie 3. Always try to get sellers to carry back or do a lease option or some other creative strategy

Truth: They say more millionaires have been created out of real estate investing than any other business. I don't think most of them sat around trying to figure out the most creative ways to structure real estate invented by gurus. They tend to be people like my dad, who had other professions and income, know a good deal when they see one, buy it with a mortgage or—if they can—all cash, and hold it for a while. I've just taken the same process and adjusted and put it on steroids. Instead of buying a house every couple years, I buy a couple a month. Most sellers as well as most buyers don't know what you're talking about if you talk about "seller carryback" or them "holding the note" or "owner financing" or what a "subject to" is, and will look at you funny. You're already overcoming a major hurdle just winning their trust enough to have you in their home and agree to deal with you.

I think this "creative" nonsense just makes it more difficult. However, it has its place. As do lease options (seller to a buyer with them giving you a down payment and then monthly payments so they get to own the house; this is usually done in crappier, cheaper areas where it's hard to get good renters and many buyers don't have good credit). Doesn't really work well in my market.

These creative strategies have their time and place. My issue is not that they are taught. I think the problem is they are *over*-taught. Just as double closing is *under*-taught. You have too many people chasing pre-foreclosures, and not that many going after "free and clears." It's just what the gurus emphasize, and the herd follows, so certain segments or concepts get saturated.

Bottom line is this: You do not need weird, creative financing that the average person, even the average real estate agent, does not understand. You just need to find a good deal, below market value. Buy it and resell it at a profit. Or hold it for cash flow and appreciation. Sometimes you will rehab it. Sometimes you will wholesale it. If it's a higher-end area, you can make more on it. If it's a higher-end area and can be improved, that's even better. The key is the property and the price.

With all this said, I admit in another part of the section that I should be trying to get seller financing more often. But myself, and most investors I know who are very successful, rarely if ever employ these tactics I am constantly reading about in the real estate forums and hearing gurus espouse.

Lie 4. You should only deal with "motivated sellers"

Truth: This one probably irks me the most. I try not to use the term myself. What is a motivated seller? The implication is that the person is desperate. Most gurus teach people to go after people who are in pre-foreclosure, where there was a recent death, divorce cases, bankruptcy, tax delinquency, and so on. I have no problem with the ethics of this, but you do not need a motivated seller in this case. I have gotten many great deals from sellers who owned their home with little or no debt, lots of equity, had plenty of money in the bank, and were doing just fine. Very few of them had any sense of urgency about selling. They were fine to wait another year. I didn't offer some fancy financing, they didn't need "fast cash" like so many bandit signs proclaim ("Fast Cash for Your House" is probably the most popular one, clearly targeting the broke and desperate).

I am telling you that most of my deals were not motivated or in any kind of financial desperation or hurry. So what made it work? They were *reasonable* sellers. I do not need a motivated seller; I need a reasonable one. Someone who is unreasonable, someone who tells me, "I want to come see your office before I will even think of dealing with you," or, "If you pay me twice what it's worth, maybe I will sell to you," or, "I will put it on the market, and if you can beat the best offer, I will sell it to you," is not someone I can deal with (these are all actual quotes, and I get them regularly). They are *un*reasonable. Someone who says, "Well, if you pay me the fair market price and I can stay there a few months, I'll consider it," is not motivated, but they are reasonable. I can often do a deal with that person.

Again, I have done pre-foreclosures and short sales and inherited property, but the vast majority of my deals have been people who are not in any kind of hurry to sell or financial difficulty. So this "motivated" stuff is way overblown.

But you know what doesn't get enough coverage? Motivated *buyers*. Think about it. We, as investors, are on both sides of a transaction. Unless we are buying to hold long-term as a rental, we are going to be selling the property in the near future (either wholesale or retail).

How motivated are the buyers? In some submarkets within the Bay Area, buyers are extremely motivated, and investors will often pay full market value for a property, especially with development potential (to remodel or add to it or tear down and do new construction). This lets you pay closer to the market price when you are buying, knowing your buyers will be motivated. Sometimes, you move to an area just a few miles away, and the dynamic is totally different, demand is not so strong. I will gladly work with a reasonable seller, regardless of the circumstances—even with no hurry or desperation on their part.

THE IMPORTANT AND UNIMPORTANT

What to focus on and what not to focus on.

No:

Your appearance.

Sometimes I dress nice, sometimes I am kind of sloppy. Some days I am clean-shaven, sometimes I don't shave for a week. I've been thin, and I've been overweight. I don't think any of this has made anyone sell or not sell or buy or not buy a property from me. In fact, since I emphasize the fact I am a private buyer, and *not* an agent, I don't want to look "too" professional.

If I walk into someone's house wearing a three-piece business suit and carrying a briefcase, I'm sure they'd be taken aback, thinking, "Whoooaaa ... Who is this guy? Too slick, too salesy." Building rapport is important when meeting with sellers. How you look or dress is not something to worry about much.

"Trappings" like an office or business cards, and so on

I have never had an office, and have no plans to. I've had maybe two or three people (out of thousands of calls) ask to meet at my office. Those were also the type of people who would probably never sell me their house. People rarely ask for my business card. I had some made; I'm sure they're around here somewhere. It is good to have business cards, but it's not a big deal. You definitely don't need an office, staff, et cetera, unless you start doing more than a hundred deals a year and are making millions. Why create overhead that doesn't really help the bottom line? I work from home or from my car, or from wherever I am with my iPhone, to send e-mails and make calls. I meet sellers at their home. I meet buyers at the property or in a coffee shop. I meet agents at their office. No one expects me to have an office. People get preoccupied with these details, instead of what really matters: getting leads consistently, evaluating them, and structuring them for maximum profit.

Making friends (in business)

I think it's important to build rapport, and create and maintain business relationships, which can overlap into friendship. I've celebrated my birthday with my business partners, and have been invited to their weddings. But it's a business relationship first and foremost, and it's important to remember that. I have helped people make millions of dollars, and then got hurt because I never felt gratitude in return. I gave up deals I wanted because I saw some partners as friends, and the loyalty was never repaid. I hired friends to help me, paid them, and they flaked on me.

Business is business, and friendship is friendship. I blame myself for forgetting that, and for letting emotions cloud my business judgment. They may overlap, but you should realize, when it comes to money, people are extremely selfish and things like loyalty and gratitude cannot be expected. Where money starts, friendship ends. For some, this is obvious. For myself, being of a generous nature, and looking for emotional validation when I helped someone make a lot of money, these were tough lessons to learn. What you should expect from your partners/investors, though, is to be honest, reliable and responsive.

Yes:

Staying on top of market trends.

Nothing is more important than being aware of the almost constant changes in the marketplace; which areas are hot, which are not. In the Bay Area, for example, a few years ago, Oakland was considered a war zone. A crime-ridden area where many houses could be had for about $100,000 and no one except the lowest socioeconomic classes wanted to live there. I'm talking only three or four years ago. In the past two years, many middle-class young professionals have been moving from San Francisco to Oakland, as they can afford a lot more property there.

It's like being compared to Brooklyn (San Francisco being "Manhattan") in a positive way. A lot of clubs, dining, and entertainment venues are moving from SF to Oakland as well, attracted by cheaper rents. These two phenomenon—cool stuff coming to town, and hipsters moving there—are feeding on each other. Prices have doubled or tripled in the last few years. Homes in some neighborhoods are selling for hundreds of thousands above asking. What is the new hot area? Who are the typical buyers? Who are the typical sellers? (So you know who to market to).

What are the best strategies to use now? For example, I had never done a short sale until I happened to come across a potential one in my parents' upscale neighborhood. That's the only reason I did it. Up until that point, I was told they are too hard to do. When I finally did one, in early 2011, I got a great deal for several hundred thousand dollars below market value. I have since bought about 10 short sales, making six figures on a number of them. But short sales were rare before 2008, and are becoming rare again with the rising market. You don't want to come to a party too early or too late. Do your research on what's trending. What areas as well as what types of deals.

Always testing new ways to market, and being aggressive in your marketing.

Massive and consistent efforts get the best results. Massive *and* consistent. Someone asked me once how I get deals. I said, "Well, a few things, but I do a lot of direct mail." She then said: "Really, that works for you? I sent out 50 letters last month and I got nothing." I was flabbergasted. It's incredible that people expect to get results from weak and inconsistent efforts.

I send out thousands of letters every single month. Some months, I don't get any deals from the letters, even with that (but I have other things working for me too). Some months, I might get one, some I might even get two. I wouldn't even expect one call from 50 letters, let alone a deal. Direct mail response rates are measured in fractions of 1%. That means typically less than one in 100.

It's also important to test different marketing pieces, such as postcard versus letter or Internet marketing versus buying leads, and so on, to see what works best. Invest more where you are getting results, and less or none where you are not. But always leave some room in your budget for new ideas and methods.

Companies like click2mail.com and yellowletters.com and others that service the industry have all kinds of mail pieces. So far, I prefer plain letters in a business envelope, but I have tested, and will continue to test, different ones. And I plan to keep trying all kinds of different marketing methods in general, and seeing what works. Some marketing works in some markets but not others.

For example, I have tried bandit signs in higher-end areas, and had no luck with them. On top of that, I got called by the police saying I will be fined $500 a day if I don't remove them (I did). I know investors who swear by them. There are so many types of marketing, as we discussed previously. But in different submarkets, and for different demographic groups, there are different ones that may work.

Never stop networking.

Many business relationships, just like friendships, can ebb and flow. Someone is your main investor, or deal provider, and then they stop producing or buying, or run out of money, or have some personal problem, or you have a falling out, whatever. I am proud to say two of my biggest investors have been with me since almost day one. I think it's good to have a few key long-term relationships in this business. But it would be a big mistake, just out of loyalty, to not make new relationships as well. This was one of my biggest mistakes during the downfall, being overly dependent on the same two investors I just mentioned.

You should be networking to meet new investors, new agents, business partners, developers, lenders, etc. Unlike marketing, this doesn't have to be done every week. A few solid new relationships a year is plenty.

Never stop learning.

Real estate is a vast field, and no one person can possibly know every niche. Imagine discovering another income stream within real estate that could bring in an additional six-figure income or a higher ROI (return on investment) than you are currently getting. I am learning about mobile home parks and self-storage now for these reasons. There are tons of books and online articles out there, as well as classes. But I've also discovered something else recently: podcasts. These are free recordings, often interviews, you can listen to on your phone or online. I've listened to many great real estate podcasts and there are literally thousands of hours of great content, and more comes out every week.

Some of the ones I have enjoyed are BiggerPockets, Tucker Merrihew's Real Dealz, Justin Williams House Flipping HQ, Brian Haskins (he has one of me on there), and Real Estate Investing Mastery. I am sure there are a few I am forgetting, and other good ones out there I have yet to discover. Search for "house flipping" or "real estate investing" and you will find loads of them. Biggerpockets.com is also a good website for learning and potentially networking. And there's a Facebook group called "Living the dream!" run by some fellow named Jason Buzi . . .

In summary, there's an ocean of knowledge out there. I even find it overwhelming myself at times. The good news is that much of it is free, and it's at your fingertips. Always be learning, growing, improving.

Speaking of new niches, here are some real estate areas I am learning about. I haven't invested in them yet, but they seem to be very lucrative. I will probably invest in one or more of these in the near future:

Senior housing, self-storage facilities, billboard rentals, mobile home parks, flipping motels/hotels.

FOOD FOR THOUGHT

1. It is your life, and just as you would be wise to structure a deal for maximum profit, it is up to you to structure this life you've been given in a way that gives you maximum benefit. What does this mean? We all have 24 hours in a day, and we all have multiple skills and multiple weaknesses. I know that right now, there are people with higher IQs than I, who have no less skill, working some dead-end job they hate, barely making ends meet.

They may have dreamed their whole life of going to Europe, but have never been out of the country, because they couldn't afford it or were afraid to go anywhere alone. At the same time, we know there are stupid people living a dream life. So it's not about intelligence or ability per se (though these things generally are good to have). What's it about? Fear, and failing to plan, as the quote alluded to earlier.

You can design a life where, after a few years of hard work, you are financially free. Then you can live wherever and however you want. Your time is the most valuable thing you have. Having money can give you more control over your time, and more free time (if you use it right; remember, it is just a tool—there are rich people with businesses and assets who literally work themselves to death and never take vacations). So money can give you more control over your time. But every day, we trade our time for money, forgetting that it is time which is more precious. All the money in the world won't buy you more time. Ask a wealthy person who is dying of cancer. If you're 20 and broke, I will gladly trade all my money for your youth, if we can figure out a way to do that . . .. I would also like it even better if I get to keep the knowledge I gained along the way, much of it from making mistakes when I was young like you.

2. Put together a mission statement. Here is an example I heard last night from an interview with Anthony Bourdain, the famous chef and TV host: "Am I having fun? Am I surrounded by people I like? Am I proud of what I am doing? Do I have anything to regret when I look at the mirror tomorrow?" I assume he wants the first three to be answered "yes," and the final one to be a "no."

There are many mission statements out there. Being businesspeople, I suggest putting something there about financial goals. Let's be realistic.

Business, any business, can be fun at times but can also be quite stressful at times. If it were only about having fun and being with people I like, I would hang out with my girlfriend or my friends at the beach all day.

3. There's a lot of talk about what to put into your body. Definitely important. But just as important, in my opinion, is what you put into your mind.

Hardly anyone talks about this, though. Are you surrounding yourself with negativity or with positive energy? The people you spend time with, what you read, what you listen to on the radio or watch on TV, how you decorate your home or office, even the music you listen to—these and more all affect your mood and mind-set. Are you dwelling on all the negative news out there or reading about success stories and getting excited about what is possible?

I love reading about people who started from scratch and created successful businesses, or people who overcame adversity. I would much rather focus on that than listening to one more person complain about the economy or how expensive things are. We are not helpless sheep. We have a great deal of control over our own lives, even if not on world events. But guess what? Even during hard times, there are people who are happy and doing well. And even during the best times, there will always be plenty of people who will be miserable and complain.

4. Help others—after doing everything to make sure you are financially comfortable, not when you're worried about next month's bills and expenses. More accurately, I would say being financially comfortable means you have enough money saved

in cash or liquid assets to survive for a year or more with no income.

Sadly, that is a better position than most Americans are in. Ultimately, the goal of everyone reading this should be financial independence, where you never need to worry about any bills or expenses ever again. You have enough in assets and/or generate enough passive income to never have to work again. That should be a top priority in life.

Many have achieved this through real estate, including myself, and so can you. Once you are comfortable, I have found nothing more rewarding than helping others. And studies have shown that of all the things we can spend money on, what gives us the most fulfillment and joy in life is giving to others.

One of my best life experiences was volunteering in West Africa. It really showed me what a difference I can make in the world, and to not take things for granted. I would give out a piece of candy, and kids would be fighting over the wrapper I just threw in the trash. More recently, I helped feed thousands of people through donations to Feeding America and by sharing the link with others through social media.

I would have never been able to have this amazing experience or give back to thousands of people without the financial success I have been able to have through real estate. Once you make it big—and if you follow my advice and principles, I'm sure you will—please remember to give back to those who are less fortunate.

By the way, I encourage you to be generous with money you make through your business when you can afford it. This could be helping the needy, but also celebrating a big deal you closed by taking a few close friends (or a dozen, as I did) out to dinner.

Or throwing a boat party. I do all these once in a while, and it's fun. But *do not* be generous within your business. I talked about how much making that mistake cost me. When hiring people, when selling a property to someone, or coming up with a partnership arrangement, et cetera, it's about the bottom line for them, believe me (I learned this the hard way, multiple times), so it had better be about the bottom line for you too.

This is your livelihood. This is your future and possibly your family's. Being generous in your personal life is a lot cheaper than being generous in your business. I would much rather take you out to the fanciest restaurant than sell you a house for $100,000 less than I can get on the market because we're friends. Don't mix up the two.

Finally, do yourself a favor and review the 10 success principles in the beginning of this section from time to time. I wrote these as a reminder to myself. I also wrote myself another reminder list, which you may find helpful in trying to maintain balance:

Read this only when you're struggling: Every successful person has gone through struggles, setbacks, and pain. Remember that it's only temporary. Have the right attitude, be disciplined and positive, and you will bounce back. Now is not forever. Stay strong and keep the faith.

Or:

Read this only when you're doing really well: You arrogant bastard! Don't be so full of yourself. It could all disappear tomorrow. The most important thing is not your possessions, but your health, your loved ones, and the person you are. Don't let a little success go to your head.

Or:

Read this only if you're doing "okay": Why are you only doing okay? Why are you not using your God-given talents and abilities and the tremendous opportunities that exist for you to be truly thriving, like so many people who are not as smart or talented as you? Have you lost your motivation or your focus or become a defeatist? Get a hold of yourself and, to borrow a phrase, be all that you can be! There is no excuse not to.

I wish you all the success in the world on your real estate adventure. You can truly create the lifestyle of your dreams through real estate.

Believe me, I know!

5

LIFESTYLE DESIGN

What do you want? You want to be rich? What if you made millions of dollars, but had to work 14 hours a day, six days a week? Does that sound good? Not to me, and probably not to you, either.

I know of someone who did this and died of a heart attack in their 40s, no doubt brought on by the stress. Let's be honest: We all want money. We need money. We want it because of the things it represents: freedom, security, opportunity. The ability to help others. Being able to spend time with loved ones. Living life on our own terms. In this book, there is a lot of information on how to make money in real estate, which I believe for the average person represents by far the best chance at financial freedom and wealth.

But this book would be incomplete without talking about lifestyle. That would be like having a car full of gas, but having no idea where you're going.

I've always hated alarm clocks; the general concept of having to go to work and do something as directed by a boss seems less natural than falling asleep and waking up again whenever you feel like it.

Most people awake to an alarm clock so they can stew in traffic jams or crowded public transportation before they're even awake. Then at the end of the work day they drowsily repeat the process in reverse!

This lifestyle represents a form of servitude, not freedom.

We've all heard the question: "What would your perfect day be like?" But a better question would be: "What would your perfect *average* day look like?"

Because some might consider getting crazy and using cocaine or doing something equally dangerous as "perfect"—but it shouldn't be aspired to.

My perfect *average* day would consist of waking up when I want, reading a newspaper, watching a little TV, and then maybe strolling to a cafe or movie—along the way making a few calls or doing a little paperwork. All without needing to ask permission from anyone.

Chances are, my free time isn't like yours. This morning after writing this, I'll go read the paper for an hour without going near a desk. I might meet some friends and enjoy lots of fun and freedom. Of course, others might choose to hike or spend time with their kids or play golf.

I also like to travel and maybe get some entertainment at a casino. What's most important is for each of us to own our time and freedom.

In other words, on a daily basis, we should have all the free time we need—and the money it takes to fully enjoy it!

Money is always good to have as long as you use it right; a good life is not about working *only* for money, but to have both pieces in place.

Try to build a business that gives you an ideal lifestyle.

Today is Monday morning. That can only mean one thing for me: movie day! Half the price and none of the crowds.

My favorite gift to give people who work with me or for me is travel. My virtual assistant from Poland, who had barely left her country before, just got to spend two weeks in warm and beautiful Thailand as her annual bonus. When you give people money, they'll usually spend it on bills or things they'll soon forget; they may not even *want* to use it. The gift of travel, however, creates lifelong memories.

It's incredible—and incredibly sad—to observe people living their lives in total fear, never taking the actions necessary to live a great life. They settle for mediocrity instead. Your struggle sucks now, but your eventual triumph wouldn't be as sweet without it.

You may be young now, but someday you'll realize that time and freedom are your most important possessions—and you've been just giving them away!

LESSONS LEARNED

Here I want to talk about different business and life lessons I have learned along the way.

I once met with a seller who began shedding tears at the thought of selling the home she'd grown up in and raised her kids in. It wasn't a distress situation at all. In fact, her home is worth about $2.5 million and is owned free and clear. Beyond being better people, we are better investors if we can appreciate the strong emotional attachment many people have to their homes. Build rapport and make them look forward to the bright next chapter in their lives.

Once you have your marketing piece and mailing list figured out and working, why not ramp it up and send out two or three times as many letters? Got your networking figured out? Then do more of it. These things aren't the same for everyone, but my point is do *more* and do *better*, or in a few years, you'll be kicking yourself over the millions in potential profits you walked away from.

There's a very obvious and powerful online marketing strategy that only one or two other people in my market are using—out of thousands of real estate investors and with billions at stake! Crazy! Seems like people just want to do what others are doing, what they've always done, or what the gurus teach.

I've been shocked about what's attracting dozens of offers and what isn't. My market is constantly changing, so I adjust my marketing accordingly. Most markets change at least once a year. Pockets that were hot become cold and vice versa. Strategies that used to work become less effective or completely ineffective. Make sure you change with the markets or you'll be left in the dust, as irrelevant as a telegraph operator.

Business/real estate isn't for everyone, I guess, so let's talk about education and jobs. I have a friend who immigrated to this great country from our Cold War adversary, Russia. She came here at age 20 and will always speak with an accent. She graduated with a business degree from a below-average school. Doesn't sound that great so far, right? She wasn't sure what she wanted to do exactly after college but ended up getting a job in human resources.

Another friend—who was born and raised here and always did very well at school—decided at an early age to become an attorney. She went to great schools, including Berkeley. She became an attorney and got a good job.

These women are now in their mid-40s. The Russian earns more than $250,000 a year as a "compensation consultant" (basically telling companies how much they should be paying their employees . . . maybe she told them how much to pay her).

The lawyer makes only $100,000 a year—which, in the Bay Area, is like making $40,000 a year anywhere else in the country.

The lawyer gets a somewhat better retirement package, I think, but neither has ever been unemployed or affected by the recession.

So is success all about education in the job world?

I'm being rhetorical. Of course it isn't.

Recently, a very successful developer friend of mine spoke at the local real estate club. One of the things she said was that when she was starting out 10 years ago, she offered to work for an investor for free just to learn. No wonder she's now a multimillionaire. Not many people have this positive, entrepreneurial attitude, being willing to work hard in exchange for learning opportunities.

I know people who only invest in their own neighborhood, within a couple blocks of where they live. And they do fine. I know other people who flip nationwide who also do just fine. I guess I'm somewhere in between as I invest in a major metro area, with millions of people.

My friend "G" worked for years in the corporate world, got an MBA, and eventually co-founded a company based on someone else's idea. He's now the CEO. The company, in the tech field, is doing very well and keeps growing.

I had a heated discussion with two other mutual friends of G (who wasn't present), about whether G can be described as a pure entrepreneur. I said that is someone like me who'd rather work for themselves and make $50,000 than make $100,000 working for someone else. Someone who can't stand the thought of having a boss, and is always trying to do their own thing. Not someone comfortable working in a corporate job for many years, but when it's convenient, jumps to a start-up or even co-founds one.

When what you're doing got tough, you walked away. Or ran away. You didn't step up your game and try harder, learning new things, or exploring new approaches, you just . . . walked away.

I understand. I've been there myself. Believe me. Not too many years ago, I was at a crossroads and almost went back to Asia to teach

English—a dead-end job that got me $20,000 a year, with novelty that quickly wears off.

But I decided to stay and fight and built myself back up. I struggled and sacrificed. For a couple years, I didn't take any vacations or even watch TV. I just tried to get back on my feet and out of the hole. I decided not to walk away like I had so many times before. And it was worth it—so, so worth it. I'm glad I made that choice.

Are you a fighter or a quitter? They're both inside you. It's your life, your choice. You're the one who will have to live with the consequences. Choose wisely.

For example, even after I got another successful investor on the phone to convince my cousin in Florida what's possible in real estate, he still didn't seem to believe it. Mindset is indeed the biggest hurdle most people have to overcome.

Rookies build buyer lists. Experienced investors build relationships.

Rookies try to make a fast buck. Experienced investors try to add value.

Rookies market the way they read somewhere. Experienced investors constantly test and innovate.

Rookies quit when things get hard. Experienced investors adapt to changing markets when things go south.

Rookies swear by formulas they read or heard about. Experienced investors know that different approaches are needed for different markets.

Rookies complain about the lack of deals. Experienced investors know there are always opportunities—some found, others made.

Rookies don't spend money on marketing. Experienced investors know that money properly spent on marketing will return five- or ten-fold.

Remember: 90% of the people you meet in this business will prove to be a total waste of your time. I was just reminded of this by an e-mail from someone who used to be an agent and now sells water (!) when he isn't sending me and the rest of his list some lame e-mails. He has never gotten me a lead and never will. I went out of my way to meet him: a total waste of my time. Unfortunately, you can't always know who will become a waste of time and who won't.

Make the best of the 10% or so who will be helpful to your business, and disregard the rest.

When you need to borrow $1 million to buy real estate, it's amazing how easy it is. When you're broke and need to borrow $1,000 to pay your rent, it's amazing how hard it is.

Every decision is an emotional decision, but trusting your instincts and experience can make it more successful. Have you ever watched the television show *Shark Tank*? Kevin O'Leary has the role of the "mean one." In my favorite episode, a young man gets emotional as he talks about how he needs the business to succeed so he can marry his girlfriend. Then something no one expected happens—Kevin is moved to tears. Does he invest? No. He says: "I was moved by your story. But I don't invest emotionally. I don't believe in this business." You have to separate your emotions from your business decisions. I learned this the hard way, and it cost me millions.

I once met a young bank teller—a recent college graduate—when I was sending wires to buy two properties. He expressed an interest in getting into real estate. I gave him my e-mail and he followed up by listening to my podcasts and asking a couple of questions. Here's what I wrote him in response:

Since you are new to this business, let me start with an overview before getting into the answers to your questions. By the way, I see you joined my "Living the Dream" Facebook group. That's good. I suggest you go back and read some of the older posts, as you may find them helpful. I am also going to post this reply there, without even your first name, as it may be helpful to others.

As a novice to the real estate business, you need to know the good news and bad news.

I will start with the bad news:

1. There are hundreds of thousands, if not millions, of people like yourself who think real estate will be their path to fortune and freedom. Some, like you, are in their 20s, and can already tell they don't like the corporate world. Others maybe are in their 40s and sick of their job or find themselves without one. The reality is that the vast majority will not make it in real estate. They will fail and go back to their job or another job.

   I've had so many people flake on me that I have stopped mentoring people personally unless they are willing to do the hard work and prove themselves.

2. You're showing up very late to the party. From 2010 to 2015, the market here in the Bay Area started making a strong recovery. We saw double-digit appreciation and multiple offers on most properties. In the first few years, 2010 to 2012, it was relatively easy to buy properties at a discount (through short sales, foreclosures and direct from owners) and you'd be selling them to a heating up market.

3. At some point between 2012 and 2015, buying at a discount became more difficult, but you still had very strong demand.

It's became clear recently that the market is slowing down. It depends on the type of property, of course. When this starts to happen, sellers still have high expectations, but the market does not reward you. For example, I am talking to a seller now in the Peninsula who wants $2.4 million for her home. A year ago, I could have made that deal happen. Right now, I can't. Same with a short sale I got in San Jose a couple months ago. There are multiple other examples.

Now, the good news:

1. Even though most in this business will fail, it's their own fault. If you educate yourself and if you are determined and persistent, you can beat the odds. If you are willing to knock on thousands of doors and make thousands of phone calls to help me find deals, I would be willing to coach you. If not, you're on your own and I wish you the best. There's a lot of good information out there, and a lot of it is free. Bigger Pockets, Facebook groups, podcasts, and so forth.

2. Even though the market is slowing down, there are *always* many opportunities in real estate. It's just the nature of opportunities that changes. For example, a few years ago, I was doing many short sales. Now, I rarely do any—maybe one a year. New construction projects were big a couple years ago. Now, not so much. I use many unique strategies to invest.

3. Contrary to popular belief, it takes no money to make money in real estate. There are multiple strategies where you can make money with no money of your own.

Now to answer your questions:

You should attend local real estate clubs and network. Some are better than others, so I can send you a link to an upcoming meeting in San Jose.

You can also do a lot of networking online through various real estate forums.

Agents make a commission when we buy a house. It's actually less work for them to not put it on the market and have to prep it and sit at an open house for days. And sometimes, it's not even their listing, but one they just know about. We try to buy it off market.

You only need a real estate license if you're representing a buyer or seller in a transaction. Not to represent yourself as an investor. I don't suggest getting one, unless your goal is to become a real estate agent. Being a real estate agent isn't any more secure than being an investor, as it's a commission-only job. And you have to kiss ass and there's office politics. We have no guaranteed salary as investors, but work on profits.

I know wannabe investors who are broke. I know agents who are broke. I know investors who make six and seven figures. I know agents who make six and seven figures. It comes down to whether you want to drive around clients and kiss their ass and work in an environment with others or whether you want to be a "lone wolf" and evaluate deals and do what makes sense. I prefer to be the lone wolf. If you don't want to be an agent, I strongly suggest you *do not* get a real estate license, as it will open you up to liability if you become an investor.

Hope this was a bit helpful.

An agent whom I work closely with wants to buy a house that I was probably going to list with him for himself. And he wants to pay me nothing over what I am getting it for! I sent thousands of letters and dealt with the hate calls and dead-end leads to get this deal. I've been dealing with the difficult seller for almost a year now. Not fun. Now the agent wants it for free so he can live there? And it's well below market, of course. Would he list a house for me for free?

Work smart *and* hard! I got started in real estate in 2005. It wasn't until 2013 that I first made $1 million in a year, and it has been going up every year since. What breaks my heart is I now know I could have *easily* done that from 2006 on, with just a few simple changes to my business model.

One small example: Double closing instead of getting assignment fee checks. Have you ever heard of a $400,000 or $500,000 assignment fee? I've seen people post assignment fee checks for $2,000 to $5,000. But having your buyers lined up, thus eliminating the risk, and using transactional funding to double close, you can make six figures on a deal, as I have multiple times. I had never started using these strategies until a few years ago.

I went to the bank yesterday to send a wire for a house I'm buying, and the teller helping me with the wire congratulated me and asked if it's my first house. When I explained that I buy and sell houses for a living, he asked me a couple questions about it, and then talked about how he is moving to San Antonio, Texas, because he can't afford to buy a place here in the Bay Area.

He was born and raised here, and doesn't want to leave, but just can't afford it. Not on a banker's salary.

I felt bad for the guy, though I did have to wonder: Did he ever really invest the time and effort in trying to figure out how he could increase his annual income to $250,000 or more? (Probably the amount needed to buy a decent house in a decent area around here these days.) Did he try to learn ways to do that, or did he just resign himself to mediocrity? Either way, it's sad. When I suggested he didn't have to go as far as Texas, that there were affordable areas just a couple hours away, in places like Sacramento and Stockton, he mentioned that his sister moved to Stockton and there were three murders in her neighborhood in the past week. He said his friend who moved to Sacramento also complains about the crime rates.

So ask yourself: Why do you want to become an agent and not an investor? Do you enjoy schmoozing with people and customer service, or do you prefer working alone? That's the main difference, as the other skills are mainly the same and so is the income potential.

My very first year in real estate, 2005-2006, I did really well. I made about $300,000 wholesaling. I'm doing a lot of the same things now, but there a few small changes. Yes, just a few small changes have taken me to seven figures. Sometimes, all it takes to make a massive impact on your bottom line are a few small changes. What small changes can you make now that could double or triple your business? Ask yourself.

Here are my own "small changes":

Learning to do more than just wholesale (JVing, double closing, rehabbing).

Expanding my territory.

Marketing more aggressively.

There are a couple more small changes I could make now that might double or triple my business again, such as working more on my marketing and my buyers list.

What needs to be done better to increase your business by an order of magnitude? Ask yourself today and act on the answers right away.

INVESTOR MANTRA

I won't allow myself to be pressured, manipulated, cajoled, sweet-talked, or harassed into buying a property I don't want to buy; paying more than what I believe is a good price; or selling for less than a profit that is in my best interest. Whether the person applying the pressure is a friend, relative, investor, agent, colleague, or any other relation.

I will do my utmost to act rationally and in my own best interest, seeking to preserve relationships when possible and desirable but remembering that my goal in business is to maximize profit, not please people.

I don't work for a living. I do deals for a living. It's a lot more fun.

What do you think of this approach?

The more money you have, the harder it is to get a huge return. I can easily double $1 in a day (buy some cookies and go door to door until someone buys them for $2). I can fairly easily make 10% on $1 million within 60 days (buy and rehab or double close a house). But I can't double $1 million in a day (without gambling and risking losing it all). And I doubt I could make 10% very easily on $1 billion in a short time. I'm reading about all these struggling billion-dollar hedge funds which made me think of this.

How would you get a good return on $1 billion? Or even $50 million?

Over the last few days I was hanging out with people who make $2 million to $20 million a year. None have advanced degrees, and none came from money. Some barely graduated from high school. Meanwhile, I know many people with advanced degrees who can't afford to buy a house.

It's all very interesting, and somewhat confusing, because it goes against what we've been taught. I remember getting my master's degree, and sending out all these résumés, and getting nowhere and feeling like a loser. I never felt like a loser making money in my own business, I can tell you that.

The world is changing very quickly, and it is filled with opportunities and pitfalls. As iconic management guru Peter Drucker once said: "Results are gained by exploiting opportunities, not by solving problems."

The future belongs not to the formally educated, but to those who innovate and think creatively—to those who capitalize on opportunities and put systems and processes in place.

6

HIDDEN CASH

One thing is certain: *Hidden Cash* was the craziest experience of my life. And I have not had a boring life.

I've lived in three countries and traveled to more than 70. I've worked as a bartender in Finland, an English teacher in Taiwan, and a real estate agent in New York City. I went skydiving in California (threw up while doing it), paraglided in Nepal, and narrowly escaped a massive riot in Kenya. I went scuba diving in Tahiti (and threw up while doing it) and whale watching in Iceland (and threw up while doing it).

But no question about it, *Hidden Cash* was the craziest experience of my life.

In a little over two months, I went from being anonymous to the lead story on *Inside Edition*, being interviewed by Anderson Cooper on CNN, and appearing on *The Wall Street Journal*'s front page. From no Twitter account to more than 700,000 followers.

Here is the inside story of this craziness.

Overall, I have no regrets. It was a once in a lifetime experience that also brought fun and joy to thousands of people. And based on some of the e-mails I received, it actually restored some faith in humanity, because there was kindness with no ulterior motive.

I hope this will entertain and inform people.

There seems to be a growing interest these days in exploring how social media can bring people together in a real-life way. This is the story of one approach that had very powerful results—and was lots of fun.

GIVING BACK IN A FUN WAY

"Be careful what you wish for. You just might get it." –Unknown Origin

Hidden Cash started on an impulse in the spur of the moment, eventually setting off a chain of events I could have never foreseen.

In May of 2014, I closed a big real estate transaction with a six-figure profit. After several really good years following many past struggles, I wanted to give back to the community, so I made a list of charities to support. But I also wanted to do something that could bring people together in a fun way.

The wheels started spinning.

I had traveled around Asia doing Coke and Mentos "geysers" for large crowds. My good friend Yan Budman had organized water balloon tosses in San Francisco. I had been organizing boat cruises with magic performances on the San Francisco Bay for friends and *their* friends. I also love reality shows like *Survivor* and *Amazing Race* and game shows as well.

A combination of these led to the *Hidden Cash* idea.

The city I love, my home, San Francisco, has been the birthplace for many incredibly fun and creative projects and social activities—including many high-tech start-ups such as Twitter.

Once or twice a year, I meet a small group of close friends and we rent a vacation house for the weekend, usually by the beach. One weekend I organized a "*Mini Survivor*" type contest that would challenge two teams of strangers. As on TV, every time a team lost a challenge, they would have to vote someone out. The winner would get $5,000 or $10,000 (donated by me).

This could be a fun way to bring people together, but my friends said it was too complicated. So one night in May, after dinner in San Francisco with a few friends, I was driving Yan home and talking to him about some type of fun activity to throw together.

We had recently tried to give a homeless man money, which he refused to take.

I said, "What if we hide money and give people clues to where it's hidden?"

Yan said, "That might work."

"And then we create a website and update it with the clues."

Yan said we should just use a Twitter account for that.

I said, "Twitter?"

Actually, I had never really used Twitter at that point, but it made perfect sense, since we'd need to instantly communicate short clues to followers. We finally came up with @hiddencash as our online handle.

I went to an ATM and withdrew a few hundred dollars. We immediately hid between $300 and $400 using some Scotch tape we picked up at a store.

It was almost midnight and we were both tired, but I told Yan I was eager to do more than just talk. We drove around looking for hiding places in Hayes Valley and the Mission District.

Yan suggested most of the hiding spots. We taped a few bills to a bike rack outside the offices of "The Bold Italic" blog, put some in potted plants that hung nearby, outside a yoga studio, and a few other random places.

I drove Yan home and then got home myself around 2 a.m. and went to sleep.

GETTING MORE MEDIA ATTENTION THAN WE EVER EXPECTED

When I woke up the next morning, several hundred dollars were hidden around San Francisco, and our Twitter account had no followers. We always intended to remain anonymous, but I did post on a couple of Facebook groups about the account. In hindsight, this was unnecessary and one of the mistakes that may have compromised my anonymity.

Regardless, it gave us a few followers, including someone who we think found most or all of the money we hid that first night. There wasn't much interest, regardless. Then I wrote to The Bold Italic anonymously from a *Hidden Cash* Gmail account to tell them we'd hidden some money in various spots around San Francisco, including just outside their office, and wondered if they wanted to do a story about it.

So we did an e-mail interview, and the story was online within two hours. Almost immediately, by Friday afternoon, we had a few hundred followers. We hid more money around the city that day and over the weekend: on parking meters, at the beach, in a laundromat, at the park.

Within 48 hours of our launch, we got picked up by major national media. I don't remember who the first was, but our number of followers blew up. Within a few days, several things happened that we'd never expected:

1. We were contacted by major national and international media, including *People* magazine, CBS News, the BBC in London, French and Japanese TV, and many others.

2. We acquired hundreds of thousands of followers.

3. We spawned hundreds of copycats.

4. We were contacted by Hollywood studios about a possible reality show.

This was all this within a few days of our late-night, last-minute idea to hide a few hundred dollars around San Francisco and tweet about it. The experience was surreal, and about to become even more so.

On Monday, I had to go to Los Angeles for a real estate conference. I had decided that I would do some *Hidden Cash* events there. I was driving down, and stopped in San Jose on the way. I coordinated with a local TV station to do an interview, not showing my face or giving my name, but showing my hands and shoes as I hid money. Then they filmed people running around looking for it and finding it.

I hid money in a few places around San Jose and tweeted clues. One was taped to a fire hydrant across from SAP Center where the Sharks play. A couple were in trees across from the Greyhound bus terminal. I met with the reporters and did an interview outside a strip mall, then taped up envelopes stuffed with cash and sent either a photo and/or verbal clue of the location to our Twitter followers.

One was hidden on the back of a stop sign in the parking lot. Another was taped behind a dumpster of a restaurant. I did this, did the interview, and then gave the news the locations, so they could wait and film it. I stuck around for a bit to watch the frenzy, before doing the long (about six hours) drive to L.A.

Dozens, if not hundreds, of young people showed up and were running around trying to figure out the locations. I could see that we'd started something that got a lot of people excited, just as we had hoped.

At the same time, in some ways, *Hidden Cash* very early became a victim of its own success. The more people are likely to show up, the more you have to think about location choices and safety considerations. Hiding money on a street corner fire hydrant or parking meter is not a good idea when hundreds of people might be headed there. This confusion only lasted for a few days, thankfully

With so much public interest and media contacting us in those early days, getting attention was never an issue. It was more a question of who to talk to, and what to say or not say. Early on, I had agreed to an exclusive story with CBS News. Mostly because a producer contacted me that first weekend and was very persuasive and sweet in the initial phone conversation. Part of their requirement was that I not do a lot of interviews. Actually, I don't think they wanted me to do *any* other TV interviews. Their story was going to air after a couple weeks on their Friday night news program and on their Sunday show.

Looking back, I should have never agreed to this. It was a promise I couldn't realistically keep, nor would it have been a good idea to do so with so much interest. Every time I did an interview (still anonymously, no name or face) the CBS producer would call and yell at me and say I lied to her.

It felt a little like I was dealing with an angry girlfriend, constantly trying to calm her down. In the end, my name came out and the CBS piece never aired anyway (they were going to keep me anonymous too). But this drama just added another layer of stress when I had more than enough as it was. With so much interest in those first days, doing any kind of "media blackout" didn't make sense.

Then, as I was watching the news not long after that, one of my favorite stories happened: Tatiana, a 14-year-old girl, had found the envelope taped to the bottom of a palm tree.

Usually, we would place $50 to $100 in an envelope (or Pez dispenser, or sugar packet). But this time, we put more than $200 in the envelope. Tatiana was literally crying tears of joy, saying how much the money meant to her, and she would send it to her sick grandmother in Mexico to buy medicine.

It was a reminder that, even though *Hidden Cash* was a game, and I like to say "it's not about the money," for some people it really *is* about the money. Even $100 or $200 can make a big difference in many people's lives.

To get an idea what a crazy time this was, you can Google "Empire Center Burbank Cash" and see some of the news stories. *Hidden Cash* was only a week old, I was still anonymous, and there was a media frenzy.

A LOSS OF ANONYMITY

I was in L.A. when my mom texted me: "Are you *Hidden Cash*?"

I was thinking about writing a long reply, but didn't yet have the time to do it. Then on Sunday, I woke up to some frantic text messages from my dad: "What are you doing? I'm shaking. Think about your family. You are destroying everything."

He'd woken up early to watch a French Open tennis match, and flipping channels, came across a CBS News report about the Burbank event. I later watched that news clip, and understood his concern. In it, a police officer worried about the crowd getting unruly; they showed people climbing the bus stop near where I hid some money, and overhead shots of a large crowd running. I was concerned too, and after that event, we stopped doing drops in parks, or on beaches, or strip malls.

In the news segment, they showed a brief clip of me being interviewed. No face or name, but my real voice, my hands, my shoes.

Obviously, a parent doesn't need to see a face or name to recognize their own child.

I wrote an e-mail to explain everything to my parents and try to calm them down. They are very private people, and don't like any publicity. They had concerns about *Hidden Cash* from the start, as did some other family members. I assured them I would do everything to stay anonymous. Unfortunately, that was a promise I couldn't keep. Less than a week later, my name was revealed.

While I was in L.A., I called the *Los Angeles Times* to tell them about the location of one of the drops.

The reporter I spoke with said, "I know who you are."

I said, "Well, you might, but you can't report it."

She said she never agreed to that. I said I spoke with her colleague a few days earlier with the agreement to keep me anonymous. She said she knew nothing about this. I asked to speak with her editor. He said he couldn't promise anything, and that there is no more privacy in the age of Facebook!

I started to panic, and asked him why he would do that.

With hundreds of thousands of people following me online, with people thinking I have large amounts of cash on me, and with my parents already freaking out, I really did not want my name out there. I asked Yan to call and tell them we were a movement with a number of people, and to please not release any names.

It worked—at least for the time being.

A few days after returning from L.A., the tabloid TV show *Inside Edition* called and e-mailed me saying they were tipped off that I was Mr. Hidden Cash. I lied and said that I was only marginally involved. I figured that was better than an outright denial, if they had some evidence. I also e-mailed them from the *Hidden Cash* e-mail account saying, "Jason Buzi is only marginally involved."

In hindsight, I probably should not have responded at all. I definitely should not have called them for an interview, which I foolishly did. They did a voice test, and matched it to previous interviews (I had already done several on TV and radio, with my real voice, but not name) and to podcasts of Jason Buzi, and got a voice expert to say that with 99% certainty, Jason Buzi was *Hidden Cash*.

They pulled various photos of me from online sources and ran the story as their lead. It was the story about me, followed by President Obama, followed by Hillary Clinton. It's one of those things you can look back at and laugh, but it certainly wasn't funny at the time.

What did this mean? Would I lose all privacy? Did I need to worry about my safety? How upset would my family be? How would this affect my ability to have a normal, private life?

I am a very private person who wants to make a positive impact on the world, but also does not enjoy being bothered. I didn't know how this would affect my ability to continue that. For the first few days, I stayed at my girlfriend's house. Going out, I wore a baseball cap and sunglasses, two items of clothing I never wear normally.

Those first few days were the worst. A reporter for the local NBC affiliate, who had been texting me since the beginning, asked for an exclusive interview after my name came out. I knew that if I was going to do an interview, to set the record straight and officially come out, it wasn't going to be with a local station. Hidden Cash had already been covered extensively in national and international media. This was no longer a local story. Of course, every reporter wants a scoop—in this case, an exclusive interview. I've learned that reporters can be charming and even flirtatious one moment, then aggressive and nasty the next.

Angry at my refusal to grant her the first, exclusive interview, she threatened to smear me and then did. She pulled every negative piece of information she could find on the Internet, from Cash Tomato to a spam article that went back almost 20 years. She, of course, ignored anything positive, like me volunteering at a library in Africa or tutoring immigrant children here, or my past charitable donations and work. She e-mailed me a few questions, then spun them in the most negative way imaginable.

For example, she asked me if I planned to monetize *Hidden Cash*. I replied that I had no plans to make money from *Hidden Cash*. She then wrote that I refused to rule out making money from *Hidden Cash*.

It was journalism at its worst, and was very vindictive, all because I wouldn't grant her an exclusive interview. Other local media were very negative as well. They republished old stories and complaints about my real estate methods.

As I've explained, I often buy houses directly from the owners, and for obvious reasons, real estate agents don't like that. A small minority of owners, especially in more affluent areas, also don't like being solicited about selling their home. Since I market in a large volume and consistently, I get noticed more than others. That's how I get deals. That's also how I irritate some people.

A couple other news outlets republished claims that I "took advantage of struggling homeowners during the foreclosure crisis." If only they knew the facts, or *cared* about the facts! During the crisis, I was struggling too, and I was not even a homeowner yet. At one point, I was staying in a rent-by-the-week motel, because I couldn't qualify to rent an apartment. And it's never been how I make my money. It was a sad reminder that so much of the media only care about sensationalism, not about the facts.

There's another phenomenon in the media, one where a young and attractive female reporter will be sent to interview a subject, often being super sweet to them. Then the final report might be very negative. Even before *Hidden Cash*, I experienced this when a local reporter got in touch to interview me about my real estate activities. It was her story that was picked up on by some of this initial negative attention.

In addition to all this, as soon as my name came out, my phone was flooded with calls from strangers from around the world, asking me for money. The same happened with my personal e-mail.

I screened calls and deleted those messages, and I would have probably changed my phone number, but I rely on it for business. The e-mails requesting money continue to this day, years later.

All of this began the weekend my name came out. It was overwhelming and very stressful. My parents were on vacation and said a news van went to ask our tenants if I lived there. A reporter left a note at my parents' house. They started getting calls and letters too. Being very private and conservative people, it was extremely hard for them, and for my girlfriend. It caused a strain in our relationship, and made me feel terrible that they'd been dragged into it.

I began thinking that *Hidden Cash* was all a mistake, and that "no good deed goes unpunished." I had spent so much time, energy, and money doing something fun for people, with no profit motive whatsoever. Now I was being accused by the media of being a scumbag who took advantage of people, and at the same time, I was being harassed by total strangers to buy them cars or houses.

MAKING THE BEST OF IT

I knew the only way to move forward was by moving forward, not hiding out or ending *Hidden Cash*. My name was out there, and to get the focus away from me personally and back to what we are doing, we had to keep doing it. Doing more and bigger. So I decided to do an interview with the media outlet of my choice, while doing more drops in other cities.

CNN has always been a leading global news channel, and being a fan of Anderson Cooper, I decided to do my first "no longer anonymous" interview with him.

After prepping for him to grill me and rehearsing answers to hardball questions that might come my way, it ended up being a two-minute, light interview. I also used it to announce new cities: Houston, Chicago, Las Vegas, New York City, and Mexico City. It turned out that except for NYC and Mexico City, we got very little traction or media attention.

Vegas, which was the only place outside California that I ever did the drop myself, was a bust. Local media and residents had little interest, as the promise of "free money" is hardly a novelty in Vegas. In addition, I spent so much time on the Vegas drops that what was supposed to be a much-needed weekend away with my girlfriend became all about *Hidden Cash*. In Houston, almost none of the money was found, and it was reported by several people that a park worker got most of the money when he showed up to work early that morning. Chicago was mildly interested.

Only NYC and Mexico City got us tens of thousands of new followers each, and lots of international media. Still, we surpassed half a million followers that weekend, got positive media, and the focus on me diminished somewhat. Things were moving forward, although the rate of growth had substantially slowed down.

I decided to expand *Hidden Cash* overseas. London—large, cosmopolitan, English-speaking—was an obvious choice.

We also did an event in Malaga, a city in southern Spain, which is the hometown of my Spanish friend who did Madrid's Hidden Cash event. This was during my second trip to L.A. It was a hectic week, where I had many drops, meetings, interviews and so on. I was barely eating or sleeping (and these are my two favorite activities!). With the time difference, I was supposed to stay awake until a little after 1 a.m. my (California) time for the clues to Spain. I fell asleep about half an hour before. I woke up a few hours later, fully dressed, and realized my mistake.

People in Spain were not happy.

I had been contacted by several Hollywood studios early on about the possibility of doing a reality TV show. Although I was never sure I wanted to pursue this, I decided to go to these meetings.

Some of these studios were household names, but I found out that the entire proposition was a big "maybe" wrapped in an "if" packaged on a "someday."

But most of the drops went really well.

And then there was Whittier. That did not go well.

Suffice to say, I felt it necessary to issue a public statement which read, in part:

"We had many events with large crowds but no negative incidents. That in itself is remarkable. Think about it—a large crowd assembled in one place for the purpose of finding a limited amount of money. Obviously, that has some potential for things to go wrong. Our followers deserve a lot of credit for being responsible. The vast majority participated in a fun and friendly spirit, in which this was intended.

"We had great events at the beach, where people searched the sand with their kids, at parks where they went out with their friends or made new friends, and literally around the world. In London, one searcher said you never chat with strangers in London, but he was making new friends as they tried to figure out the clues together.

"We are proud to say that, for the most part, our activities brought people together, in a spirit of cooperation and friendliness, not competition and greed. More than the money, I think people were—and are—hungry for a way to use social media to connect with others in a real life way. I think this is why *Hidden Cash* has grown so quickly and attracted so many followers. Most of us love our social media, but we also want to connect and do things together in real life.

"And then there was Whittier. . . . We planned to do seven events over four days in the Los Angeles area. There was only one person in charge of selecting the venues, preparing the drops, hiding the money, contacting media, tweeting out clues, retweeting winners, etc. Every drop takes hours. This doesn't count traffic, and time needed for other activities like eating or sleeping. Things go wrong. Having barely slept in days, I fell asleep half an hour before I was supposed to tweet out clues for Spain. Riverside was hours late and not the best venue. Doing a drop at a small park in Whittier after dark was probably not the smartest idea. A large crowd turned out, and things got rowdy. Young men yelled obscenities on live TV. Sprinklers were broken, plants were trampled, fences were mangled. The city estimates the damage to the park at $5,000.

"Today I spoke with the city manager, Jeff Collier, who was very cordial, and I offered to pay this amount to compensate for damage to the park. I will be sending a check tomorrow for $5,000. Not knowing

L.A. County well and feeling the pressure to do so many drops in a short amount of time was not a good combination. Going forward, we will learn from this. As the crowds are big, event locations need to be selected even more carefully than we have so far, perhaps in consultation with local authorities. Night-time events have a different energy, and as fun as they can be, we may suspend those for now. Other events all went very well, including those in 'poor' parts of town, like East L.A.

"Putting this one unfortunate incident aside, we want to emphasize how much we have enjoyed exploring the various parks and beaches in L.A. County and all the places we have visited, and how many of our followers wrote that they enjoyed the time spent with friends and family in the various parks where our events have taken place. And that they discovered or re-discovered some wonderful spots. We think overall we have actually done a lot of positive in encouraging people to enjoy the outdoors. California in particular is blessed with so many wonderful city, county, state, and national parks. We must treasure and respect these. That's an important message, and part of the reason we are paying to restore William Penn Park in Whittier, CA.

"Our movement has grown, and has given us a lot, but also taken a lot from us in terms of time and energy, not to mention money. We are a couple guys, not a big organization, and we don't have unlimited wealth either. Frankly, we are at a crossroads. As we figure out what's next, we thank you for your support and understanding. This has been a wonderful experience, and we hold our heads up high, and so should the vast majority of our followers."

GETTING READY FOR FINAL DROPS

There was another consideration—Yan's name hadn't come out yet. Although he was ambivalent about it at times, I was personally anxious for his name to be out there.

There were two main reasons. One was, I thought he deserved credit for his role in *Hidden Cash*, and since he worked in marketing for social media, it is related to his career. The second reason was more selfish: I didn't like all the spotlight on me personally. Especially when my name first came out in the media, *Inside Edition*, and all that. It would have been better if the world knew/thought *Hidden Cash* was two or more people. By the time his name *did* come out, it didn't matter that much. But I am still glad he got credit, and the attention he got was very positive. I think Yan exudes more charm and charisma than I do. He is a naturally outgoing person, whereas I am an introvert.

He is good at winning people over with his personality, whereas I tend to come off more serious and, at times, arrogant. So he did great in his interviews before we pulled the plug on *Hidden Cash*.

Yan met with a reporter from TechCrunch, an influential tech blog with millions of readers. I think it was a month or more after the meeting when the story finally came out. We couldn't have asked for a more positive story about us and the movement we started.

You just never know. That's one thing I've learned many times about the media. It doesn't matter how friendly the reporter is, what their demeanor is, what you tell them, what the facts are—they will write the story they want to write. Using the same set of facts, one journalist will portray you as a saint, and another as a villain. Whatever they think will make a better story, or based on their personality, or mood that day, or God knows what. It's always a crapshoot. But TechCrunch was great.

DECIDING WHETHER TO TAKE THINGS IN ANOTHER DIRECTION OR QUIT

In the week leading up to the finale, some smart people I knew and respected helped me realize that the only way to make *Hidden Cash* sustainable long-term would be to turn it into a business.

I met with those smart people and brainstormed ideas.

Do we develop and launch an app to do *Hidden Cash* virtually? Everyone argued against that, saying it would take too much time and money to develop a good app, and unless you could get millions of users, it's not a business. You'd be competing against games that cost $10 million to develop. You would spend many months and hundreds of thousands of dollars dealing with various technical issues to develop an app.

The other way to keep *Hidden Cash* sustainable was to take on sponsors. We had been approached by a few, from a casino in New Jersey to an ad agency that wanted to promote a popular Discovery Channel show to a Japanese game maker.

I grappled with this for a while. After thinking it over, and a lengthy discussion with Yan, we decided the right thing to do was to end *Hidden Cash* on a high note, preserving its legacy as a force for good in the world, and not try to turn it into a business or anything else.

CALLING IT QUITS

On August 12, 2014, we issued this statement:

> *They say all good things come to an end, and for us, we realize that time is now for this phase of @hiddencash.*

What started as a fun project to bring a smile to people's faces, bring people together, and perhaps inspire them to pay it forward, took off beyond what we ever expected.

Seeing how much fun people were having made us keep going—taking it to cities all over the United States, and even Mexico and Europe.

Our events brought together hundreds of people at a time. Best of all, we got to hear so many inspiring stories about how Hidden Cash was making a positive difference in people's lives.

We saw a 14-year-old girl in tears because the money she found would help her sick grandmother buy medicine. A man wrote that he gets depressed watching the TV news every night with his wife and son, but since we started, they have a reason to be happy while watching the news, seeing how people are coming together in a fun way. A young lady who found our money just handed it over to a little girl who was looking. A young boy gave his to the homeless. People said they were inspired to buy groceries and gas for those in need. A woman wrote that her daughter read about us, and decided to give her savings to the needy. A young man in London said you never talk to strangers in London, but he made new friends as they tried to figure out the clues together.

These stories and the hundreds like them touched our hearts and made us feel a sense of responsibility to our followers.

Your stories have kept us going.

We ended up spending more time, energy, and money on HC than we ever expected to. It became more than a full-time job. But it's also been extremely gratifying.

We realized at one point that the only way to continue HC was with sponsors, and we were approached by several big names.

After much consideration, we decided that turning HC into an advertising business was not in line with our goals and mission.

So, we have made the difficult decision to end the HC money drops.

What started May 22 on the streets of San Francisco ended on August 3 on the beach in New York City.

This does not mean we are abandoning our mission of bringing people together in a fun and positive way, or of giving back. If anything, we are more determined than ever to keep doing that, reinforced by the love from our fans and witnessing firsthand what a positive impact can be made. It does mean that this phase, of money drops in public places, as we have been doing it, is over. It is simply not sustainable for two regular guys to keep doing this forever.

We feel a real sadness at ending this phase. We will miss many aspects of this—the fun of planning the events—but mainly, seeing so many smiling and happy faces, of all ages and backgrounds coming together. We will miss that. But although part of us really wanted to continue, to return to cities that showed us love, and come to more places around the world, we realized that HC could not be sustained forever, without turning it into a sponsored business, and we did not want to do that.

Since HC started, hundreds of independent, local versions have sprung up. From Mexico City to Vancouver to San Diego to the UK, others have been inspired to do something similar. If they can do it in the spirit in which it was intended, and safely, we support what they are doing. Nevertheless, we want to be clear we are not affiliated with any of these. We commend those who have good intentions and good planning. If done safely and for the right reasons, this is one way in which the HC movement can live on and grow around the world.

Although we are saying goodbye for now, and ending this phase of Hidden Cash, please stay tuned, as we hope to do more fun and giving things in the future. We are also interested in hearing from you. Whether it's for ideas of what to do next, sharing your stories with us, or wanting us to speak about our experiences and the lessons from Hidden Cash to your organization. Contact us by e-mail at officialhiddencash@gmail.com.

Most of all, we hope we have inspired others to believe there is goodness in the world, to give back when they can (which doesn't have to be financially), and to believe in their own power to make a difference.

If two regular guys from San Francisco were able to bring joy and excitement to thousands worldwide, it is our sincere belief that anyone can do the same, and that people tend to underestimate their own strength and ability—to change their own lives, and to change the world.

We also want to thank you. In reality, it is you who inspired us. It is you who gave the intangible gifts of the stories and smiles, and shared them with the world.

Thank you to all of our followers.
Love,
Jason Buzi and Yan Budman
Founders, Hidden Cash

7

PHILANTHROPY

I believe in long-term thinking and balance. There's lots of greed among real estate professionals, so I'm constantly dealing with many greedy people. To keep a sense of balance, it's critically important to practice some form of philanthropy.

I love doing real estate and I love the money it brings me, but I want to use that money as much as possible to do good and give back to people. Hopefully the following stories will inspire you to undertake regular philanthropic activities and achieve real balance in your life too.

1. Poland

In 1997—just after receiving my master's degree in economics from Cal Poly Pomona—I wanted to gain good travel experience while doing something to give back to others for all my blessings.

So I joined the nonprofit Volunteers for Peace program and traveled to Gdansk, Poland, to spend a few weeks volunteering as an English tutor in a summer camp for third-grade kids. While there, I also traveled a bit around Europe and became friendly with other teachers.

(Poland has been conquered many times over the centuries, but the people are so very warm and friendly that I've returned there many times to see old and new friends; I am planning another trip.)

Then a few months later, in 1998, I became involved in the international Odyssey of the Mind creative problem-solving competition involving students from kindergarten through college—held that year at Disney World in Florida.

I wanted to invite the seven Polish students I'd recently tutored, but they couldn't afford to participate at a cost of more than $1,000 per student. I couldn't afford to pay that, either, so I organized a fund-raising effort.

A local cafe was owned by a Polish national, so I talked to him about my idea and he introduced me to a lady who was also willing to get involved. We went around to Polish churches and organizations. We gathered lots of small checks there, and several hundred dollars through a stockbroker. We raised more than $10,000 in about one month.

After they went home, I kept in touch with the students and one of the teachers, named Kinga. A few years later, she and her boyfriend came to the U.S., so my volunteer experience led to lifelong friendship!

Then, years later, I was in contact with a former student, Monika, who was having financial problems. She told me she was about to lose her apartment. At first, she wouldn't accept my money, but finally did, and after sending her a couple of gift amounts, I hired her as my virtual assistant. I still pay her $750 a month and she's paid her way—helping me get several new business deals. My support is no longer charity and our relationship continues 20 years after I first went to Poland as a volunteer.

2. Volunteering at a library in Ghana

I have always felt drawn to volunteer in Africa because everything goes so much further there, so any effort has much more of a positive impact.

In 2004, I decided to go to Africa and volunteer in an English-speaking country that had a stable government. A Canadian friend had lived in Ghana. She read books to children and was very surprised to learn that the country had no public libraries.

So she converted an old ship container into an impromptu library facility and opened it on land donated by the city of Accra. Adult literacy classes are also offered there.

I only volunteered there for a month, but made many friends—some of whom I've stayed in touch with.

The heat in Ghana can be quite severe, but its friendly people and laid-back (even "sleepy") atmosphere make it worth a visit. From Accra, the country's coastal capital, to the dusty northern towns of Tamale and Bolgatanga, near the Sahara Desert, Ghana is considered safe, relatively quiet, and stable.

Ghana generally suffers less from crime, corruption, and political instability than its neighbors and other nations in sub-Saharan Africa. The country may be a good starting point for anyone interested in learning more about this huge and mostly-poor continent.

For example, after returning from Ghana, I have continued to send donations to some of the children I met there. In response to a $200 gift, I received a thank you letter that said, "Now I have enough to live on and attend a year of school."

That's about what I pay for a good dinner with my wife. So there's absolutely no reason not to give the same amount where it's needed.

3. Two other causes in Africa (Congo and Ethiopia)

I actively support Mavuno, a faith-based social enterprise in the Democratic Republic of the Congo (DRC) that focuses on rural development through asset-based and participatory strategies. I have met with board member and former veteran Mike Myatt, who has worked with a Congolese community organizer he met in Korea to improve the lives of people living in Africa's poorest country by establishing agriculture schools there.

I also donate to San Francisco-based Tangible Hope Foundation, which currently sponsors 50 young girls in Kofele, Ethiopia. Programs include helping these girls, and hopefully more in the future, to attend school, improve their hygiene and nutrition, and attend after-school programs. According to their web site, "Tangible Hope strives to empower young girls in order to realize their full potential and to help put an end to the social norms in Ethiopia."

4. For one school year, I volunteered at a San Francisco Bay-area elementary school, helping some of the 24 students with their homework.

The students—most from immigrant families—had trouble following the language and academic subjects. I was so struck by how many of them obviously needed more attention, I remember thinking that the class could easily have used five of me. Despite our best efforts, many students were obviously slipping through the cracks and would find it difficult to finish school, much less find work and acceptance in mainstream American society as adults.

In order to help them keep their spirits up, I would sometimes bring ice cream or pizza for snack time. When one of the students had a birthday, I also organized a piñata party.

After volunteering for a year, I made donations to the foundation that sponsored this praiseworthy volunteer program.

5. Major donor to the San Francisco Botanical Garden
I have always loved going to these gardens on nice days and walking around. In order to increase involvement in worthwhile local organizations, I made a donation and a brick was inscribed with my name!

8
REFUGEE NATION

Is there a major global issue you care about? Do you think you're too "small" to make a difference? Think again. If you have an idea that is unique and relevant, you can start a movement and make news around the world. This can have a huge ripple effect. How do I know? Because I recently did it.

In 2015, I started reading more and more about the refugee crisis. This humanitarian disaster has existed for decades. Recently, it has reached epic proportions, with thousands drowning at sea while trying to flee war zones to Europe and other perceived "safe havens." It's been capturing headlines.

Yet, as far as I could tell, no one was proposing any real solutions to the crisis. I had an idea years earlier for a homeland to be established, where any refugee from anywhere in the world would be welcomed and be a free and equal citizen (currently, the vast majority of refugees don't get citizenship and are unable to work at all or are barred from many professions). Beyond discussing my idea over the years with a few friends, I had never done anything.

In 2015, with the crisis making news around the world almost daily, I decided the time had come to publish and publicize my proposal.

I created a website, wrote an e-book, started a Facebook page, and hired a PR agency to work on getting media.

In July, my PR agency was able to get me an interview with *The Washington Post*, one of the country's most influential publications.

That led to more interviews and articles in media in the UK, the European continent, Australia, and beyond.

Although I may never live to see my admittedly ambitious proposal become a reality, it stimulated a lot of discussion and debate about finding solutions to the refugee crisis.

We all have a historic opportunity to address and hopefully resolve what is arguably the world's largest, most urgent humanitarian catastrophes—the swelling tide of refugees sweeping every region of the globe.

In 2015, I finalized and received extensive media attention for a Refugee Nation proposal that I had originally suggested almost 10 years earlier.

Here are pertinent excerpts from my proposal, along with links to several online resources and media coverage:

CRISIS AND SOLUTION

"The world's population has never been wealthier, healthier or more connected. Yet the number of people displaced has never been higher" - *David Miliband, former UK foreign minister and President of the International Rescue Committee*

There is a humanitarian crisis smoldering in every corner of the world. This crisis has been growing for many years; finding a viable solution has never been more urgent.

It isn't climate change or other, better-publicized crises. This crisis doesn't receive the attention and response it deserves because it primarily affects the world's most powerless, needy, and vulnerable population.

Once you know that millions of people suffer day-in and day-out without hope, and that it is in your power to save or greatly improve their lives, wouldn't you want to support a viable solution?

Millions of victims of this manmade crisis are left to face the lethal consequences of full-scale wars, armed conflicts, government upheaval, and ethnic cleansing. All without any consistent, effective help.

Frequent news reports touch on the hundreds of thousands of people forced to flee their homes due to conflict, or the thousands who drown at sea while desperately seeking a better life.

On World Refugee Day, June 20th, 2014, the UN's refugee agency reported that the number of refugees, asylum seekers, and internally displaced people worldwide has, for the first time since World War II, exceeded 50 million people.

Think about it: that's 50 million people uprooted and forced to flee their homes. It includes:

- Syrians escaping their civil war.
- Christians and Muslims running from ISIS atrocities in Iraq and across the region.
- Ukrainians fleeing their nation's conflict with Russia.
- Palestinians barely surviving in refugee camps.
- Sudanese persecuted for their faith.
- Congolese displaced by civil war.
- Burmese minorities affected by government policies and natural disasters.
- And countless others in every region of the world.

They come from all backgrounds, races, and religions. They struggle in every corner of the world.

There's one common denominator: these innocent individuals, families, communities, and even entire ethnic groups, have been left homeless and stateless by armed conflict, economic turmoil, and ethnic cleansing.

So this proposal was made public on World Refugee Day, 2015, in order to say: Enough is Enough!

We are committed to ending this ongoing horror with a radical solution that isn't unattainable or crazy. We offer the most practical and implementable solution to the world's perennial refugee crisis.

The United Nations High Commissioner for Refugees (UNHCR), International Rescue Committee (IRC), and other well-meaning organizations—governmental, non-governmental, faith-based, and others—have spent decades trying to help alleviate the suffering. Yet the problem continues to spiral out of control, with no comprehensive solution being seriously discussed.

That kind of solution is clearly needed. The scattered piecemeal actions taken so far don't even begin to address this problem. At best, they feed some people and provide temporary shelter—for years, lifetimes, and even generations—in crowded refugee camps. These sincere efforts are commendable, but do not begin to solve the core problem.

The camps' host countries almost never offer refugees any citizenship, or even the right to work. As a result, too many displaced people resort to crime, join extremist groups, or fall victim to human traffickers.

For example, Jordanian camps house hundreds of thousands of refugees from the ongoing conflict in Syria. Wealthy older men from Gulf countries reportedly come to refugee camps and choose brides as young as 13. Their families are so desperate for a little money that they abandon their precious daughters into lives of constant misery.

Congolese refugees fleeing to Uganda have resorted to digging through garbage heaps and prostitution in order to survive.

And what of those educated people formerly employed as doctors, lawyers, engineers, or academics? Countless numbers are now unable to work and forced to waste away in tents or crumbling buildings without using their abilities.

Even if external assistance programs could meet refugees' basic physical needs, what is life like for them? It is little wonder that so many refugees suffer from depression and PTSD. How can we, as privileged citizens of the first world, allow so many fellow human beings to live in unimaginable misery?

So what can be done to address this crisis, and alleviate the suffering of so many innocent people?

One solution is glaringly obvious. It may sound grandiose, but is not only logical—it is the *only* practical solution to this persistent, debilitating problem.

Ready?

Give these millions of stateless people around the world a state of their own!

Today, 195 sovereign countries are recognized around the world. We need one more—a country that any refugee, from anywhere in the world, can call home. Where each has the same legal rights to reside, work, pursue an education, raise a family, buy and sell property, start a business, as any of us. Where everyone is a citizen, regardless of ethnic background, religious affiliation, or any other personal status. They would help build a completely inclusive and compassionate nation in which every refugee is automatically granted full citizenship.

HOW TO MAKE THIS DREAM A REALITY

There are a number of ways this dream can become a fully functional solution:

1. The number of super-rich individuals is rapidly growing. There are now some 2,000 billionaires in the world, according to *Forbes* magazine.

    If even *one* of these individuals could be persuaded to enthusiastically embrace such a cause, success would become much more likely.

    For instance, one billionaire could buy multiple islands or a vast area of land where the new nation could be created. They may even be able to help transport many thousands of the refugees to their new home. Sooner or later, sovereignty should follow.

2. The United Nations could have its most tangible success in many years of programs and relief efforts. Official support of this cause might well persuade the majority of its member nations to vote for a refugee nation to be established.

3. The United States government—the world's most powerful— and EU governments could take up the cause as a collaboration.

4. One large nation might agree to designate a major part of its property to become the world's new Refugee Nation, at little or no expense. There are many millions of acres of unused land, along with many thousands of uninhabited islands, which would be ideal for this purpose—and all are available.

5. Or a smaller nation could admit a large number of refugees as immigrants, in exchange for some form of compensation support and extensive goodwill from the world community.

6. Influential celebrities, especially those known for their human rights work, or political leaders—in or out of office—might be recruited to help the cause.

7. Millions of ordinary people could support the cause in some way. Although the average individual cannot wield the power and influence of a celebrity or billionaire, if enough of them take up this cause, it will become a reality. Rich or poor, known or unknown, we would ask for (and greatly appreciate) such vocal support.

If any of these happen, it will only be a matter of time before a refugee nation might be established, and millions of lives saved or improved.

Sadly, the groups which will probably *not* offer significant support are the obvious allies—organizations working with refugees. We will, of course, contact them and appeal for help. Yet such "insiders" tend to resist any outside solution.

Such resistance isn't limited to any industry. After PayPal revolutionized online financial transactions, its founders famously said that if any of them had come from a related background such as credit card services, they would not have thought of the idea, and would likely have dismissed it as impossible or impractical.

It sometimes takes an outsider's perspective to shake things up. And most institutions are resistant to venturing far from the familiar and upsetting the status quo. There are many examples in the business world. An upstart company named Netflix forced movie rental giant

Blockbuster to close its stores and ship DVDs to customers on a monthly subscription basis, adopting the Netflix model.

NGOs in the business of refugee relief employ thousands of people. I am not suggesting that they don't care about the people they work with, but they tend to focus on operations or logistical strategies rather than revisiting core values.

Consider my experience with Jenny, a friend of a friend and a very nice young lady, who once studied "development" or a similar major. Jobs in her specialty weren't easy to come by, so she was thrilled to land a well-paying job as an analyst for an NGO that worked with refugees. She had never seen a refugee camp or met any refugees. Hers was a purely an administrative position with an NGO that works with refugees. One that I am sure gets millions in public or private grants and donations.

In the early stages of formulating the idea of a refugee nation seven or eight years ago, I spoke with Jenny about this proposal. She quickly dismissed my idea without giving any specific objections. She just said the NGO community she was familiar with would never support it. I would have been quite happy to discuss and debate specific points with any NGO insider. But Jenny was certain that no one would even entertain the possibility.

Shouldn't a big idea with real potential to change millions of lives for the better be discussed and debated on its merits, rather than being dismissed out of hand because the established "community" isn't likely to support it?

As we have seen, despite the sincere efforts of thousands of well-intentioned and well-paid Jennys at dozens of organizations like hers, the refugee crisis is growing steadily worse and heartbreakingly tragic.

It's time to advance a radical solution based on big ideas.

The status quo is simply no longer acceptable!

Here are some useful links for more information:

RN official page: http://www.refugeenation.org

Wikipedia page about RN: https://en.wikipedia.org/wiki/Refugee_Nation

Original article from *The Washington Post*:

https://www.washingtonpost.com/news/worldviews/wp/2015/07/23/a-silicon-valley-mogul-wants-to-solve-the-global-refugee-crisis-by-creating-a-new-country/

The Atlantic article: http://www.theatlantic.com/business/archive/2015/10/jason-buzi-refugee-nation/410728/

9

CLOSING STATEMENT

I've heard a depressing statistic more than once: Fewer than 5% of people who attend a seminar or read a "how-to" book, like this one, ever take any of the action steps they've learned.

I sincerely hope that you will defy this statistic.

There are three things I believe truly matter in life:

Lifestyle, Love, and Legacy.

Lifestyle is the life you create for yourself. What does your average day look like? Are you a zombie, waking up early and driving to a job you don't enjoy, to work for and with people you don't care for, to make just enough to pay the bills but not have the time or money to pursue your dreams? This is reality for millions of people, and we are taught to be grateful we even have a job. This doesn't sound like a great life to me, and I hope I've shown you another way here.

To me a great lifestyle means doing what you want, when you want and with who you want.

This may be the only life you get. Try to create a great lifestyle for yourself!

Love is all the people you care about. It means finding your soulmate and having a great relationship with that person. It means family. It means having meaningful friendships.

Many people don't have a great lifestyle (how many people can go on a three-week luxury vacation any time they want?) but are sustained by the love in their life:

By a loving spouse, by their kids, by their friendships. That's not bad either.

But I'm greedy. I want to have it all.

Legacy: We won't be here forever. What do you want to be remembered for?

A middle-class Canadian housewife I had the privilege to meet followed her husband to Ghana, West Africa, where he got a job as an accountant for a mining company.

One day, while reading books to her children in the garden, other neighborhood kids joined to listen. She soon found out that in Ghana, almost no children have books at home. Even more shocking, libraries did not exist! She grew up in Canada reading books from the library, expanding her imagination and learning about worlds beyond her own.

And yet, these poor African children never had this opportunity. Inspired, she got a shipping container, some land donated from the city of Accra, Ghana's capital, and books and funds donated by friends back home. She has now opened libraries all across Africa, serving many thousands of children and adults. What an inspiring legacy!

You can create a legacy by making a financial or time contribution to a cause dear to your heart, by helping others, by creating something that will outlast you.

By writing a book, making a movie, recording a hit song, building a beautiful building, or a painting. Artists and writers have the greatest legacy.

We all read books and watch movies and appreciate art created by those who have long departed.

Whatever it means for you, your life will become more meaningful and greater if you try to create a lasting legacy.

We get so absorbed in our petty daily problems and concerns, and this is also a way to rise above that, to make your life greater than just about yourself.

And it feels great to give!

I hope that this book has inspired you and showed you how you can create a wonderful lifestyle for yourself, using real estate as the vehicle, and how to make the most of the time and financial freedom you can enjoy as a result. It's your life, and you are not me. You may not want to spend your free time reading *The New York Times* at a cafe.

You may not want to hide hundreds of dollars at the beach for strangers to dig up. You may not want to travel as much as I do.

But it's *your* time, and you can never get it back. You own it. If you're trading it, whether for $10 an hour or $100 an hour, unless you love what you do and the life you live, you are selling it too cheaply. My suggestion: Build a business that gives you the time and financial freedom to pursue your passions, and live the life of your dreams.

All the best on your journey!

10

INTERVIEWS WITH OTHERS WHO ARE LIVING THE DREAM

Justin Williams is a successful real estate investor and educator based in Southern California. He hosts a popular podcast at http://houseflippinghq.com.

What did you do before real estate?

I owned a satellite dish business.

What prompted you to get into real estate?

I always wanted to invest in real estate. One day a friend told me about a call where the guy was going to be talking about short sales. I didn't know what this was but by the end of the call we were signing up for a course and seminar in Atlanta, Georgia, and were on our way!

Can you give a general description of your real estate business—how it works, what you do, where? For example, mine would be, "I buy off-market residential properties all over the SF Bay Area, in different prices ranges, and either wholesale, double close, or rehab them."

I buy, fix, and flip properties primarily in SoCal and a few other states nationwide. Flip about one hundred per year.

Can you talk about your first deal? How long did it take you to "make it?"

Since we were doing short sales, we actually got several deals in the "pipeline," but didn't actually close on any until about seven months later. We made $17,000 on that first deal.

Have you outsourced or automated aspects of your business? If so, which?

Yes, the entire business is automated. I don't work with or speak to agents, contractors, sellers, or buyers. I spend about two to three hours a week working with my GM and acquisitions manager while they run the business.

What has been your biggest challenge or challenges? Could be a particular deal or mind-set shift you needed to make, etc.

Challenges are just a part of owning a real estate business (or any business for that matter). We literally buy problems. I tell my team, every day, when you wake up, put on your problem-solving hat because that is what we do. The challenges are always different. Sometimes it is finding more money, sometimes it is finding more deals, sometimes it is finding, working with, or dealing with contractors. If you don't plan on problems, this will be a challenging business for you. If you expect and embrace them, you will have a much better shot at success.

Do you have any advice for people who aren't sure if they should make the leap?

I would like to say that everyone should have a real estate investing business, but honestly, if it is something you are not passionate about, or are not willing to dedicate some time and energy into, then it really probably isn't for you. That being said, if you do want to change your life, go after your dreams, and want something more for yourself, and your family, I would highly recommend taking that leap. It won't be easy, but it sure beats the alternatives.

Describe what might be a typical day for you.

Since my real estate business is systematized, each day is different. I don't just wake up and start looking at houses or following up with sellers or go look at houses. On a typical day, I will usually wake up around 6 a.m. and I try to focus on my top one-three priorities for that day. My goal is to have my top priorities done by 11 a.m. each day, and I will spend the rest of the day on any odds-and-ends items, or just spend time with my wife, or kids, or going surfing, biking, or to the gym, etc. Usually, about once a week at about 6 p.m., I host a group coaching call for one of my coaching programs, and about once a month I either host or attend a three-day mastermind event or seminar focused on real estate or marketing. The key is focusing on the few items and eliminating the rest. This will be different for everyone based on where you are in your journey.

What are your goals for your business?

I am pretty happy with where we are with our real estate investing business and would like to continue to do about 100 deals a year. My main focus now is continuing to develop programs and tools to help others do the same with both real estate investing and business in general. Our goal is to have an annual income of $10 million by the time we are 40, which will be in about four years in 2020. We also want to continue to be a part in efforts such as supporting organizations like OUR (http://ourrescue.org/). Last year, through House Flipping HQ and our flipping business, we were able to donate $60,000 to help fund a rescue mission which rescued 16 girls being held as sex slaves.

How has real estate helped you live the lifestyle of your dreams?

Real estate has allowed me and my family to live in the location and home of our dreams, spend more time with my wife and kids, and be there for them on any and all special events in their life. It has allowed us to travel and create more memories as a family, and allowed us to serve and help others in ways we had previously only dreamed of. I work when I want, I don't report to anyone, and I go where I want when I want. I am able to bike, surf, and spend my time doing the things that I want when I want. I am able to help my parents and others who I work with. I am able to help my students achieve this same dream, which probably brings me more joy than even doing it for myself. I am living the dream and believe others can obtain that same dream if they only have the desire, get the right help, and are willing to do what it takes.

Do you do any philanthropy or helping others and, if so, what does that mean to you?

Yes, through the real estate OUR and coaching programs, etc., mentioned above. I also serve in my church and am currently assisting in the local Cub Scout organization. I help at my kids' schools on occasion as well. In fact, this morning, my wife and I are going to my son's kindergarten class to talk to them about entrepreneurship. I strongly believe it is important to teach children at a young age that they have options and can choose to create a life for themselves in the way they want and not have to follow societal status quo.

Any other words of advice?

Just know that creating a better life for yourself, your family, and the world is very doable. You just have to stick with it and be consistent in your efforts. Be willing to take the right kinds of action and be ready and willing to make mistakes and learn from those mistakes. Surround yourself with people who have been there and are on the same path as you. There are many who have come before you that you can learn from, so you don't have to reinvent the wheel. Being a successful real estate investor (or entrepreneur of any kind) is not necessarily easy, but it sure beats the alternatives, and in my personal opinion, there really is no other way.

* * *

I met Aaron Katz at a seminar. He is a successful investor in apartment buildings and puts together deals with other investors to buy hundreds of units at a time.

What did you do before real estate?

I've invested in several small business partnerships. Mostly retail. Also real estate brokerage/agent experience in single-family and multi-family. Management, sales background.

What prompted you to get into real estate?

I felt my skill set would translate well into MF. Passive income, ability to build a business from above, putting in place systems where the business could run on a daily basis without me being involved every day. As Michael Gerber said in E-Myth, working on my business, not in my business.

Can you give a general description of your real estate business?

I structure group purchases (syndicate), multi-family acquisitions, and oversee them using professional third-party property management. These investments return excellent annual cash-on-cash returns to my investors (often 10%+), and they frequently double their money in five years or less upon exiting the property via sale.

Can you talk about your first deal? How long did it take you to "make it?"

About eight months. It was a 90-unit multi-family property in Arlington, Texas. I raised $750,000 from a group of 11 other investors.

Have you outsourced or automated aspects of your business? If so, which?

Many. Daily operations are outsourced to third-party management.

What has been your biggest challenge or challenges?

I can't think of any.

Do you have any advice for people who aren't sure if they should make the leap?

Get a mentor. I lined up with Brad Sumrok [a real estate investor/mentor]. Make sure you have the personality, social skills, and leadership abilities to take this on and stay persistent with dogged determination.

Describe what might be a typical day for you.

When I'm pursuing deals, I'm coordinating the "big picture," the many moving parts that go into a large multi-family acquisition. I'm analyzing deals, touring deals, making offers, negotiating contracts, talking with investors, raiding capital, arranging financing, working through the loan process with lenders, legal document preparation with attorneys, inspections, planning post-close rehab plan, working toward a close. When in between deals, I'm staying on top of daily communication, weekly calls with my management company, holding team members accountable to performance standards, sending updates/monthly reports/distributions to investors.

What are your goals going forward for your business?

Continuing to grow my multi-family portfolio.

How has real estate helped you live the lifestyle of your dreams?

I can work from anywhere when not touring deals. I have set up systems that allow my business to run without me. Passive income. I live life on my own terms, no one else's.

Do you do any philanthropy or helping others and, if so, what does that mean to you?

I hope to inspire others by doing what I do, spread positively, let people know that it is up to us and only us, our success is determined by internal, not external, factors.

Any other words of advice?

Invest in self-education. Then leap. One doesn't need to know it all to get started. Just how to take the first step. The rest will be figured out and learned along the way!

* * *

I met Jaelin White when I attended a real estate class in Arizona. I was impressed that, as a 19-year-old, he was already doing quite a few real estate deals. All when most of us at that age were mainly concerned with being popular and getting someone to buy us alcohol.

What did you do before real estate?

Before real estate, you would have found me doing a number of things: sleeping in class (high school), selling low-quality "designer" sweatpants to other kids at school, pitching other 16-year-olds on network marketing, losing the $2,000 I saved up in the stock market, or quitting the job I had only had for a week. Yes, I was all over the place. I had known that I wanted to be rich, but had no idea how or what would get me there. I was a 4.0 GPA student, but I resented the system—get good grades, go to college, get a job, save, and live happily ever after. By my senior year, I was no longer known as the bubbly freshman that all of the teachers counted on to be the one student who actually genuinely enjoyed class. Instead, I was known as a "reject" of sorts. I began to lack interest and dedication in my classes and slacked off on homework. Instead, I found myself studying sales techniques or finding the latest sourcing company to buy fresh inventory for my wannabe clothing company. My reputation was slowly morphing into that of an entrepreneur that people laugh at until the entrepreneur succeeds.

What prompted you to get into real estate?

At 18 years old, I found out that my girlfriend's father had signed us up for the $300 "Rich Dad Poor Dad" seminar. After reading terrible reviews about the event, I wrote it off as pointless and a waste of time. In fact, the only thing that got me to show up on that first morning of the seminar was my remorse for letting Brian pay for the event. Needless to say, it ended up changing my life. At the event, I was vaguely introduced to the technique of "wholesaling." They hadn't mentioned it by name at the event, but they did mention that you could get paid about $10,000 just for finding good deals. To me, that sounded a whole lot more appealing than buying a house, putting tons of money into fixing it up, and listing it on the market. Not to mention, I was dead broke and was sleeping on my girlfriend's family's couch. So from there, I went home with a 500-page book on real estate and learned how to wholesale.

Can you give a general description of your real estate business?

I buy off-market residential properties in Memphis and Phoenix in different price ranges and either assign or double close them right now.

Can you talk about your first deal? How long did it take you to "make it?"

It was tough for me getting started because I was literally negative $100 in my bank account. I hadn't had a job and was in high school, so money wasn't something I came by all too often. I believe I started truly studying real estate in March of 2015. I dug through the books, went to local meetups, watched YouTube videos, and did anything possible to get started. I remember the first appointment I ever went on: It was to a property that had been listed on the MLS and was on Craigslist (I had no clue what the MLS was) and stated that the property "needed repairs." I pulled up in my great grandmother's 1990 Toyota Corolla and hid it around the corner from the house so that the agents would not be able to see what I was driving. Luckily, they actually ended up pulling up in an uglier car than I had! Anyway, I proceeded to walk through the property and act like I knew what I was doing. Somehow, they bought it! They were ready to write up an offer with me when I realized one very important aspect of a deal—I didn't know what to offer! Nor did I have the $500 in earnest money that they were asking for! But I did not tell them that. ... Instead, I told them that I had to meet with my investor partner and run some serious numbers on the property, but that we were deeply interested and could close fast if the numbers worked. I proceeded to leave without a clue as to what I was doing. Needless to say, I didn't get the deal. After a couple more failed attempts at getting houses under contract off of Craigslist, I finally decided to "get out there." I put some bandit signs out for a local investor who was starting a real estate school. They read "real estate investor seeks apprentice, call xxx-xxx-xxxx." Somehow, by the grace of God, there were 20 "We Buy Houses" bandit signs mixed into the 100 he gave me. I didn't know if it was an accident, but I decided to keep quiet. The next weekend, I went and put the bandit signs out on Saturday at 5 in the morning. I expected loads and loads of calls from my signs! But alas, I got none. Until that week when I finally heard the phone ring. I answered to a guy who had inherited a property and just needed to get rid of it. The "zestimate" on the property was $90,000 and he was willing to sell it for $25,000! Wow! The real estate genies had answered my prayers and sent me a motivated seller from heaven. I rushed a contract over to him and got escrow open. That was April

18, 2015. The deal was not as easy and smooth as I would have liked, but after a buyer backed out and I got a price drop to $15,000, I finally lined up a new buyer and we closed on May 18, 2015 (two days before my graduation), and I got a check for $12,118.

Have you outsourced or automated aspects of your business? If so, which?

I have yet to 100% outsource anything in my business besides my marketing. I do pay a company to do my letters and I have a guy who puts out my bandit signs. As far as a team goes, I do have a part-time acquisitions manager and a part-time dispositions manager. They help me with negotiating with sellers and buyers, getting signed contracts, and keeping all parties close at hand during the closing process. I have created processes to allow leads to flow smoothly through our systems, but have yet to fully hand that off, however, I definitely plan to have my entire business automated by the end of 2016.

What has been your biggest challenge or challenges?

My biggest challenge has been consistency. It's very important to be laser-focused on one thing that you can make your bread and butter. For me, I struggled with staying consistent with my marketing. I would set a mailing campaign, get a deal, sell it, and close it before I would ever set another mailing. This meant I'd only be doing one to two deals a month and was never able to grow! I've been able to solve that by making sure that I have a specific amount of marketing going out each and every week and by tracking my numbers so that I know exactly what's going on in my business.

Do you have any advice for people who aren't sure if they should make the leap?

You're never going to be successful watching from the sidelines. Hopefully you laughed at the thought of a shaggy-haired, 18-year-old boy going to a property and attempting to make an offer on a $200,000 house. I can guarantee that you'll be able to do what I did a lot more effectively! Just pick one thing to do and do it—whether it is to put out bandit signs, send letters, or call 100 Craigslist ads a day. Take action and you will most definitely see results.

Describe what might be a typical day for you?

Typically, I wake up right around 9 a.m. and pop up out of bed. I'll hop in the shower, throw on a white V-neck and khaki shorts, and sit at my desk in my living room to listen to some positive videos and get myself in a good mood. I'll review what I have to do for the day, see what my goals are, and adjust my tasks accordingly. To be quite honest, my days are generally easy-going. I check to make sure that I don't have any new untouched leads in my CRM system, make the follow-up calls I need to make, check on any deals we have escrow open on, make sure my team is on the same page with buyers and sellers, and get a general overview of where the business is at. Once all of this is done, it's normally around 2 or 3 p.m. I'll then go grab some lunch with my fiancée and go to the park or drive down to Scottsdale (a nice area of Arizona) to do some sightseeing. Normally, I try to be back around 4 p.m. or 5 p.m. to do some cold calling to new potential buyers and build relationships. From there, I normally spend an hour or two reading or listening to podcasts and do whatever self-development I've lined up for myself. After that, my fiancée and I eat dinner and enjoy each other's company. At around

10 p.m., I FaceTime my close friend Jake Spaulding (another 18-year-old investor out of Houston) and we catch up on the day's events in business. Yes, we literally FaceTime every single night. From there I listen to relaxing audios until I fall asleep!

What are your goals going forward for your business?

One of my main goals is to be consistent with my marketing. Thus far, I have set at least two-three mailings a month since the beginning of 2016. I'd like to do more mail and have leads flowing in week in and week out so that we have consistent deal flow. I'd also like to bring my acquisitions manager and dispositions manager on full-time to help with the increased number of leads. My monetary goal this year is to do at least $1.2 million in revenue, which I do believe we will be able to achieve with the amount of marketing that we have been putting out.

How has real estate helped you live the lifestyle of your dreams?

Real estate has allowed me to be able to live in my own home, buy my own car, and provide for myself and my family, all at the age of 19. I feel truly blessed to have found and created a business that allows me to realistically plan and expect to be making $100,000 in one month, which is double the average yearly salary in America. I do not have any set places to be, things to do, or people to impress. All I have to focus on are my family, God, my goals, and staying true to myself. Real estate has allowed me to feel truly free in a world that can be so constricting.

Do you do any philanthropy or helping others and, if so, what does that mean to you?

Giving is a large part of what makes success feel so good. At this point in my career, I have been able to give back to my family and my church—and it makes me feel amazing to know that I am able to give to others because I am financially stable myself thanks to real estate.

Any other words of advice?

Excuses are baloney! The human mind will find a million and one ways that it cannot achieve a given task, and it is up to you to prove your mind right or wrong! You can choose to rise above the noise and negativity and achieve your goals and desires— all it takes is focused, consistent action while under the right guidance.

* * *

Tony Alvarez is a successful investor and published author with many years of experience. He has seen and done it all in this business, and often speaks at real estate clubs throughout California.

What did you do before real estate?

I was working blue-collar jobs like janitorial services, night manager for Shakey's Pizza. ... I dropped out of high school in my senior year so had few prospects for much else.

What prompted you to get into real estate?

A combination of my level of desperation and the promise of becoming wealthy—I was up watching TV late at night and saw an infomercial about real estate by a guy named Dave Del Dotto. I was unemployed, married with a young son, and desperate for money. The magic words I heard that night were: "Anyone can get rich in the real estate business, you don't need money, education, good credit or any prior experience." That was me, broke and desperate—uneducated, no credit, no money, no prospects and no nothing! When I heard those words I felt hope and I was hooked!

Can you give a general description of your real estate business?

Presently, as an investor, I make the majority of my income from owning and managing small, inexpensive (under $200,000) residential rental properties like houses and one- to four-unit properties in one of the lowest-priced real estate markets in the High Desert area of Southern California.

As a speculator, I focus on buying the same type of properties, but in neighborhoods where I personally do not want to own rentals, and either fix and resell them at top dollar to owner occupants, or just flip to other investors. I find and create deals from a variety of sources: real estate agents, owner sellers, other investors, asset managers, banks, and lenders. Over the years, I have specialized in working with agents that specialize in listing distressed properties. I also partner or finance deals for other well-known, experienced investors.

Can you talk about your first deal? How long did it take you to "make it?"

My first deal I purchased through a real estate agent who had an office that was walking distance from where I was living. I bought that place within a month of receiving Dave Del Dotto's books and tapes, which I bought that night I saw his infomercial (I never did get past reading the first two chapters and listening to the first cassette tape before buying my first deal).

It was a 1920-built, two-bedroom, one-bath, 900-square-foot stucco house with a great front porch, a two-car detached garage, and not much else. It was located on Lima Street in Burbank, California. It was a fixer. The place did not even have windows, but we moved into it while doing the repairs; that way, we did not have to pay rent and a mortgage. My parents helped with the financing—we paid $78,000 and spent $9,000 on repairs (that was big money back then); we sold it for $155,000. But I had another deal in escrow from the same neighborhood, which I bought directly from an owner-seller immediately after the first and that was my start.

Have you outsourced or automated aspects of your business? If so, which?

Everything from acquisitions, financing, rehab, property management, bookkeeping, ongoing maintenance, reselling ... pretty much every step—but that did not happen overnight.

The most difficult aspect to delegate was acquisitions, but once I let go of wanting to micro-manage and control every detail, it fell right in place. Everyone is different; let them do their thing as long as you land the deal.

What has been your biggest challenge or challenges?

We don't have enough time or space to cover all of the challenges inherit in learning to deal with the details of the day-to-day decision making and all the things that can go wrong in doing this business. ... But having to choose one thing? I would have to say it's been my own self-imposed limitations and lack of understanding.

Honestly, even from the beginning, it's all been about developing my own ability to get beyond my self-doubt and conditioned level of understanding. It took me a while to realize that we are without limits in what we as individuals can decide to accomplish—the rest is just hard work.

Do you have any advice for people who aren't sure if they should make the leap?

I suppose the most important question to answer before you jump into real estate, or anything, for that matter, is: What do you want to do and why? That's a very personal question. The thing is, we have to understand what our real motive is, or motivation, for doing whatever it is we choose to do. For example, I did not get into this business because I loved it, or because I had always dreamed of becoming a "real estate millionaire." I heard a guy on TV say that any idiot could get rich in real estate and you didn't need anything but your own strong level of desire and determination and hard work to do it!

I believed it was possible to do, but more importantly, I believed it was possible for me!

Bottom line, why did I jump in: I needed the money. I saw getting rich as claiming my freedom from the stress-filled feeling of being a loser, a financial failure, and all the self-loathing that comes with it, period.

I fell in love with what I chose to do much later, when I realized I was actually doing something worthwhile. By rehabbing destroyed houses that nobody wanted, I was actually restoring neighborhoods, creating jobs, providing safe, beautiful, and affordable housing for folks that appreciated what I did. Then I was really hooked—I fell in love with becoming someone who did good, and that earned me the right to do really well financially long-term.

I liked that, and that has kept me in the business for over 30 years.

Describe what might be a typical day for you.
Nowadays, my life is pretty much the same as a shepherd of sorts. ... I just have to keep a close watch over my flock. I have learned to delegate effectively, to share and help others accomplish their goals while they help me accomplish mine.

I wake up in the morning at 5 a.m. sharp, whether I went to sleep at 8:30 p.m. or midnight. I do my personal stuff like meditate, read, walk, and get ready for the day. By 8 a.m., I'm at my desk at home—I have no other office and never have. I pay for an office which my assistant uses and for tenants to communicate with if they so desire. It costs me $300 a month including rent, phone, insurance, Internet, all of it, and it is the ugliest office in the city. I have a person on the other side of the world who was up while I was sleeping that gathers all kinds of articles on real estate and business happenings, and sends them to me via e-mail with links so I can click and read the 10% or the entire article on what's happening on the big stage. Then I review anything else that came in on my e-mail and address what's urgent, important, or trash. By then I'm ready to write for an hour or longer if the mood hits me (I have learned the value of journaling and documenting my experiences).

Then I'm free! Off to either check up on those that work with me, like driving by some of the places being rehabbed, or dropping in on real estate agents, escrow, and title company folks we work with, or the local bank, were I secure my financing (I typically bring them fruit or donuts, whatever I'm in the mood to bring, or sometimes I just drink their coffee and eat theirs). In other words, nowadays, my time is my own. But, that took many years of ups and downs to achieve.

Our goal for years has been to buy a house a week and sell one a month. We have never been looking to set the real estate world on fire or become the next Donald Trump (although I do think he would make a great president, had to sneak that in there). Purchase prices range from $50,000 to $200,000 in all stages of condition, from teardowns to a place that just needs to be cleaned before rented or resold. The biggest issue I have to deal with typically is whether I will be meeting someone for lunch or not. This is a far cry from what things were like when I first got started, when I was doing everything by myself, but, even then, I quickly learned the advantage of building a team of business friends to help me grow quickly.

What are your goals going forward for your business?
Today, it's all about maintaining what I have accumulated, and learning to improve on my own skills of managing money—much tougher than making it.

That said, I have always had monetary and material goals, but simple ones. Remember, I came to this country when I was 5 years old from Cuba. At first we were poor and things were tough. We didn't even speak a word of English. Over time, things got better, all in sequence with our level of effort.

So, I come from a very average middle-class home and lifestyle, but I'm happy.

All I ever wanted was to get to the point where I was making $10,000 a month net income from owning 10 rental houses that were free and clear—no mortgage, and no debt on anything I own. Not very complicated or sophisticated, but that's all I ever really "needed" to be free.

And because I perfected a series of simple steps that I kept (and still keep) doing relentlessly, the real estate slot machine paid off. I have been fortunate to reach my goal more than 10 times over. So, how much money does one need to make to be happy?

As much as we as individuals decide it will be.

My goal now is not really connected to a dollar amount as much as it is being of value to those I work with, and the community that has made it possible for someone like me, with all my imagined limitations, to become financially free and independent.

How has real estate helped you live the lifestyle of your dreams?
The real estate market is a huge market full of opportunity and wonderful people and experiences just waiting to be discovered and developed. Honestly, I owe everything I have accomplished

financially, and much of my personal development, to working within its broad currents.

I was fortunate to find it watching late-night television, while others pony up a couple of thousand dollars and become real estate agents, some going on to earn millions, while still some decide to get master's degrees in real estate finance and secure jobs at banks earning six-plus-figure incomes, huge bonuses, company cars, and all kinds of perks.

The real estate industry affords us a magnificent opportunity to become as comfortable or wealthy as your imagination or dreams can take you. And it doesn't care if you're poor, uneducated, broke, or miserably riddled with low self-esteem. It just asks you to make up your mind to do something daily in the direction of learning how it functions, and more importantly, to be clear as to what you will bring to the table.

Do you do any philanthropy or helping others and, if so, what does that mean to you?

Yes, but this is a very personal and private part of my life which I choose not to disclose or discuss in detail. That said, I think that while generosity is not a necessary component to becoming financially wealthy, I don't believe one can ever free themselves of greed, or the fear of poverty, which is a requirement of hanging onto wealth long-term, as well as experiencing a full and healthy life as a whole human being.

Any other words of advice?

Actually, I have learned to never give advice. However, I will make one suggestion: Whatever you decide to do, keep in mind that we only have one life. That's a fact that we are all knowledgeable of, yet we live most of our lives in denial, as if we will live forever—we won't.

And in the end, we will only have the results of our individual actions. We can make that a life full of wonderful decisions and actions resulting in worthwhile accomplishments, and a host of people who love us for not only what we've accomplished, but for who we became, and for what we taught and represented to everyone around us.

So, here is the best kept secret of success I have learn in my 60 years in this life: Learn to love your business associates. Learn to care about the success of others as much as your own.

If you do, not only will you wake up one day to realize you have become financially wealthy beyond your imagined goals, but you will have built a meaningful and wonderful life worth living.

* * *

I met Haim Mamane Palman a few months ago and was immediately impressed with him personally, as well as the fact he is living in San Francisco, but has been successfully doing deals long distance. His preferred market is Memphis, Tennessee. He manages to do all of this remotely, and also takes a lot of vacations with his family. At the moment, he is traveling in Japan, yet he put systems in place so that the money is still coming in, whether he is in SF, Israel (his home country), a beach in Puerto Rico, or visiting temples in Kyoto.

What did you do before real estate?

I was a physical security professional. I was working for the Israeli government, securing Israeli embassies, consulates, and its diplomatic staff, including ambassadors and Consul Generals around the world, as well as El Al Airlines stations around the world.

From 2004-2015, I was the Director of Security of the Jewish Community Center of San Francisco. That was my last job before getting into real estate investing full-time.

What prompted you to get into real estate?

I wanted to have a different lifestyle and to live life to the fullest—spending more time with my family and traveling more around the world. I knew that the right model of real estate investing can support my desired lifestyle and provide financial means to my family.

Can you give a general description of your real estate business?

For my active side of the business, I do mostly virtual wholesaling, double closing, and rehabbing properties in Memphis, Tennessee. For the passive side of the business, I have rental properties, partnerships with a company that fix and flip properties, private lending, and seller-financing deals.

Can you talk about your first deal? How long did it take you to "make it?"

I was in "paralysis analysis" mode for more than a year before pulling the trigger and buying my first rental property in 2011. It was a single-family home in Antioch, California, and I bought it at the bottom of the market. Since then, I'd already sold the property at a profit, but it took me a long time to make the decision to buy it and I probably looked at more than 50 properties before pulling the trigger. It was nerve-wracking.

Have you outsourced or automated aspects of your business? If so, which?

Yes, for my wholesaling business I outsourced the lead-generation aspect of it with two virtual assistants in the Philippines. I have a leads manager who handles all the incoming phone calls and e-mails, screens for motivation and book appointments, and I also have an acquisition manager who goes to appointments and gets properties under contract. The next phase is to hire a sales/disposition manager, transaction coordinator, and marketing manager, as the goal is to have a business that is run without me or with minimal involvement from me.

What has been your biggest challenge or challenges?

Overcoming fear and believing that it's possible to make money in real estate without a lot of money.

Do you have any advice for people who aren't sure if they should make the leap?

It took me more than three years to work on my mind-set and make the jump and become a part of the 2% mind-set group. There are good days and bad days as entrepreneur, and I'm still out of my comfort zone, but living life on your own terms is priceless.

Describe what might be a typical day for you.

Waking up at 5:30 a.m., working on and in the business until 8 a.m., breakfast with the kids, taking the kids to school, coffee with my wife, working on and in the business until noon, exercise until 1:15

p.m., lunch with my wife, working on and in the business until 3 p.m., picking up the kids from school, working until 6 p.m., quality time with the family, go to bed around 10:30-11 p.m.

What are your goals going forward for your business?

$100,000 per month with minimal involvement of my time in the wholesaling business. $50,000 in passive income from rentals, partnerships, and private lending.

How has real estate helped you live the lifestyle of your dreams?

Without real estate, I would not be able to spend more quality time with my family, travel to the World Cup in Brazil, Netherlands, Crete, Croatia, Costa Rica, Puerto Rico, Japan, and spend two full summer months in Israel with my extended family. Real estate has been a blessing in my life and it enables me to live life to the fullest.

Do you do any philanthropy or helping others and, if so, what does that mean to you?

Yes, I do contribute to the Jewish Community Center of San Francisco, to my synagogue, and to Metta Center for Nonviolence Education. It means a lot to us to give back, especially to institutions and causes that we believe in, and our goal is to increase our financial and time contributions as our business grows.

Any other words of advice?

You get one shot at life, do it right, make every moment count. Your life doesn't get better by chance, it gets better by change.

GLOSSARY

Absentee owners: People who own a home they do not live in, usually a rental (although it may be vacant, or have a family member living there for free). Real estate investors often target these sellers as they tend to be less emotionally attached to the property, viewing it as an investment. They can also usually sell faster than someone living in their house who needs to pack and find a place to move to. Tax records indicating a different mailing address than the property address are the easiest way to locate absentee owners. Also known as non-owner occupied (or NOO) properties.

ARV: After repair value. This is what the property would be worth after being remodeled and/or expanded. Not to be confused with FMV (see below).

Bird-dog: Someone whose job it is to locate properties, generally off market, for an investor. A property scout, they generally get paid to pass on a lead. They do not get the property under contract, otherwise they would be a wholesaler. A typical bird-dog fee is $500, almost always paid if the property is acquired, though fees may be much higher in certain markets. For example, I have paid up to $10,000 for a lead leading to my purchase of a property.

CAR form: The California Association of Realtors real estate purchase contract, the most commonly used one in California. Make friends with a real estate agent in your state and get a blank copy of the most common contract in your state. Study it, make copies, and practice filling it out. Most contracts are pre-printed with a lot of "legalese" and only a few blank spaces the buyer and seller fill out in pen and sign are truly pertinent (price, terms, et cetera).

Comps: Comparable sales. These are used by appraisers, investors, agents, and sellers to determine the fair market value (FMV) of a property. You can look up some comps through public websites like Zillow and Redfin, but agents, who have access to the MLS, can provide a comprehensive list. Ideally, comps are from the past three (max six) months, within half a mile or less, and more or less the same size and condition. Since it's very rare to have two identical properties (the exception would be a new subdivision), adjustments need to be made for condition, size and factors like lot size, busy road, swimming pool, and so on. Real estate is not a perfect science, so looking at the same set of comps, it's not unusual for two different people to draw different conclusions. Some sellers only cherry-pick the highest comps as their point of reference (the neighbor with the much larger, remodeled house) while some investors do the opposite.

DOM: Days on market. How long it takes a property to sell. I consider average DOM in any market to be a very important indicator of the strength of that market, so find out what it is!

Double close: Taking title to a property, and then selling it shortly thereafter without doing any work to it. Different from wholesaling, as you actually take title to it. This requires money, which may be your own, or a loan, or even come from the person you are selling to.

Free and clear owners: Owners of property with no mortgage, meaning they have 100% equity. Investors like to target these too, as they have more room to negotiate.

FMV: Fair market value. This refers to the *current* market value of a property, as distinguished from ARV, which refers to the potential future value.

HOA: Homeowners association. Most condos, townhouses, and some SFR (see below) subdivisions have one. It involved a governing board and monthly dues for all property owners. There are also certain restrictions which can be placed by the board. These can be very significant. For example, shortly after buying my first condo, I found out that I was prohibited by the HOA from renting it out, which was my plan. Fortunately, I was able to sell it at a profit.

MLS: Multiple listing service. This is the public network where real estate agents post properties for sale, and update the status to pending or sold. Only real estate agents/brokers can post, but once a property is on MLS, there are dozens of public websites where it can be viewed, including Zillow, Redfin, Trulia, and on many agents' websites. Unlike some investors and gurus, I don't think having MLS access is a must these days (I never have), but you want to be friends with at least a couple agents who can look up comps, et cetera, on MLS when needed. These days, there's a lot of publicly available information without MLS access.

NOD: Notice of default. When someone is in pre-foreclosure, after missing several mortgage payments, an NOD is filed. The exact process varies by state, so check your state's foreclosure laws.

Pocket listing: A real estate listing an agent knows about but has not yet been publicized on MLS. It may be their signed listing, a colleague's, or a seller they have spoken with who has not yet signed. Pocket listings can be a great way to get deals off market and below market.

Rent back: When you purchase a property, and the seller gets to remain in the house after closing. May be free, for market rent, or below market rent. I've used this tactic to close deals that otherwise wouldn't have happened. Many sellers are just not ready to leave their house yet. Sometimes they need the money from the sale to buy a new place. Use with discretion.

ROI: Return on investment. $1 million invested with a $200,000 profit would be a 20% ROI. $500,000 invested with a $45,000 profit would be a 9% ROI, et cetera.

SFR: Single family residence. A detached house.

VA: Virtual assistant. Someone who works for you but is not physically in your office. May be domestic or overseas. A VA can do tasks like sending out e-mails, stuffing envelopes, calling sellers, following up with agents, et cetera. Many investors have one. There are many websites where they can be found, including Odesk, Elance, et cetera.

ABOUT THE AUTHOR

Jason Buzi is a real estate investor and developer. He buys, builds, and fixes up houses throughout the San Francisco Bay Area. He has also invested in mobile home parks and raw land. In 2014, Jason gained worldwide celebrity and extensive news coverage as a man behind the Hidden Cash phenomenon, which sparked massive worldwide scavenger hunts in San Francisco, Los Angeles, New York City, London, Berlin, Madrid and elsewhere.